3 Steps to Your Job in the USA

Go From F-1 to H-1B

Steven Steinfeld
With Yinping Huang

ISBN: 1542656931
ISBN 13: 9781542656931

Acknowledgements

Thank you to the students from around the world who have helped make *3 Steps to Your Job in the USA* the best reviewed and most practical job search guide ever written for international students.

Thank you first and foremost to international student and IIT Master's graduate Yinping (Ping) Huang who worked closely with me on the original content and organized and led the international student focus group.

Thank you to Ron Cushing, Director of International Services at the University of Cincinnatti, who updated and expanded the *Visa Laws and Your Work Options* chapter originally co-written by immigration attorney Mark Rhoads, and Rich Cruz for updating the cover originally designed by Rayme Silverberg.

A big thank you as well to the universities that sponsor my workshops and the university Deans, faculty and administrators who have given me the opportunity to work closely with international students, especially Ann Carrel and Anthony Preston at Northern Illinois University and Ana Rossetti at the Illinois Institute of Technology.

Preface

*"I took the road less traveled by, and
that's made all the difference."*

— Robert Frost, American Poet
in "The Road Not Taken"

A few years ago, an international student referred to in this book as Ziya (Vivian) Zhu contacted me for job search advice. At the time, eight months had passed since her graduation from a Midwest Business School. Vivian was highly motivated to find a full-time marketing job with the potential for H1-B sponsorship, but she had received only two unsuccessful interviews despite applying to hundreds of jobs online.

Vivian finally secured a part-time job, but it had little to do with her education, knowledge of digital marketing and marketing analytics, or the experience she gained during her internships. Discouraged, confused and desperate, she engaged me in a one-to-one coaching relationship. By the end of six weeks of coaching, she had completed eight telephone interviews leading to five in-person interviews, and received three solid full-time job offers (two in scmarketing and one in operations). Vivian settled on a 10-month contract assignment as a Marketing Associate for a fashion firm in Manhattan. This was not her dream job, or the highest paying job that she was offered, but it promised a great learning experience and a path to both her dream job and sponsorship. Within two months after starting her new job, the company offered to promote her to Marketing Analyst and sponsor her for an H-1B visa.

Since the publication of the first edition of this book, Vivian has moved on to even bigger and better things, including two additional sponsorship offers. Vivian first moved on to a Digital Marketing Consultant position working for an affiliate of a global pharmaceutical company with a second promise of H-1B sponsorship. She also decided to obtain a Master's Degree in Integrated Communications Marketing in an evening program at a major university. As she neared graduation, she pursued and was offered her first step up the management ladder as Analytics Supervisor at a leading global media company—with the promise of H-1B sponsorship.

Vivian has been successful because she is determined to make a life and career in the U.S. for as long as she wishes. Her drive has resulted in active networking, a compelling resume and LinkedIn profile, development of impressive interviewing skills, and an excellent return on investment in the job search coaching that I provided to her.

If you follow the guidance in this book, you can be just as successful. However, if like Vivian, you need professional support in order to achieve your job search goals, please read the chapter titled *Job Search Coaching*.

I could tell similar stories to Vivian's about my clients and workshop attendees in finance, engineering, HR, research, operations, sales, international relations, and business consulting— and any other degree program or industry.

During the six weeks that Vivian and I worked closely together, her strengths, skills, knowledge, experience, work values and personality did not change, but there was a great change to her job search experience. So what was the secret to getting five in-person interviews and three job offers within only six weeks? The secret to unlocking her door to success—and yours—is the 3-step job search approach.

Over the last few years, I have introduced the 3-step approach to many thousands of professional job seekers and international students through my books, workshops and seminars. Hundreds of readers and attendees have told me that they have dramatically improved and accelerated their job search results by using the 3-step approach and the easy to follow job search strategies, tactics and tips contained in this book.

If you are wondering why you are not receiving many responses to your job applications, you will be interested to know that up to 80% of jobs are never posted, fewer than 25% of posted jobs are filled by an outside candidate, almost 50% of jobs are filled by candidates recommended by a current employee, and it's no longer unusual for a company to receive hundreds (or even thousands) of resumes in response to any single job posting.

Since receiving an interview is often the result of strategic networking, many international students see their lack of personal or professional connections, which they believe U.S. students to possess, as their main disadvantage in job searching. In actuality, relatively few U.S. students have a well-developed professional network. However, this does not take away from the fact that networking effectively is critical to an international student's job search. Teaching the international student how to network effectively in the U.S. is one very important objective of this book.

Most people would agree that international students face greater challenges than U.S. students when they apply for work (e.g. visa rules and regulations, the possibility that you may decide to return to your home country, and less familiarity with U.S. culture and language). Asking an employer to deal with these concerns requires that you significantly outperform U.S. students at your job interviews. For this reason— and because of the many insights I have gained from hundreds of mock interviews with international students—I have devoted the largest chapter in this book to interviewing skills.

I have engaged with a group of international students from countries around the world to fully adapt the 3-step approach to the specific needs of international students. This third edition of *3 Steps to Your Job in the*

USA contains valuable advice from successful international students in addition to proven guidance from top career coaches, immigration experts, and university career services professionals. It also includes many examples of exactly what to write or say that you will find easy to modify for your own situation.

Only 2 out of every 5 international students who come to the U.S. to study plan to work at an internship or job before returning home. However, in the end, 4 out of 5 decide to at least try an internship or longer term job search. This book is applicable for international students in any of the following categories:

1. New students in the U.S. looking ahead to their first internship.

2. Students planning to return home shortly after graduation, but still wanting the experience gained by one or more internships or Co-op* programs while enrolled in school.

3. Students planning to stay in the U.S. after graduation for up to one year in jobs related to their major under OPT*.

4. Students wanting to work beyond one year in the U.S. under an H-1B* visa (with or without plans to extend those visas).

* Get complete definitions and information about internships, OPT and H-1B visas in the chapters titled *Interning Your Way to a Job* and *Visa Laws and Your Work Options*.

Throughout the book, references to international students include recent graduates, and expressions such as "job seeker" and "job candidate" or "company" and "organization" are used interchangeably. I have also used mostly Chinese and Indian student references, marketing and financial industry examples, and male pronouns. Please concentrate on the content of the book rather than the word, phrase, gender, nationality, industry or career choices.

PREFACE

The information, direction, advice and guidance contained in this book applies to ALL international students seeking employment in the U.S., and contains everything you need to know to land a great internship or job— even at organizations with policies that discourage the hiring of international students.

Table of Contents

7 Ways to a Job Interview

"Choose a job you love, and you will never have to work a day in your life."

– Confucius

One job search misconception that you might have is that there are only one or two ways to get job interviews. In reality, there are at least seven ways to get job interviews, some of which will get you priority consideration. **This book will not only explain how to utilize the six best ways to get a job interview, but will even increase your chances of successfully using the traditional, <u>but rarely successful</u>, seventh approach of only responding to online job postings.**

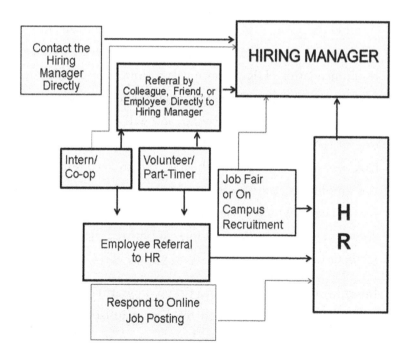

This book will not only explain how to utilize the six best ways to get a job interview, but will even increase your chances of successfully using the traditional, but rarely successful, seventh approach of only responding to online job postings.

1. The most effective approach to getting a job interview in the U.S. is to connect with a "hiring manager"* indirectly by way of a strong referral and/or recommendation from an employee, friend, or colleague of the hiring manager. The informational interview is a great way to get this kind of referral and recommendation (See the chapter titled *The Power of the Informational Interview*). A job offer is not guaranteed, but the interview is almost assured.

    *When I use the term "hiring manager," I am referring to the person in an organization who has the authority to offer you a specific position. In all professions in the U.S., this person can be either male or female.

2. Another great way to get a job interview is through an employee (in good standing) referral to the HR department, even without a strong recommendation. HR professionals assume that an employee will not bring forward a candidate for consideration less qualified than the employee doing the referring, and will often feel an obligation to give the employee's candidate serious consideration. Companies have also found that job candidates who are recommended by valued employees tend to perform better, stay longer, and integrate faster. This is why resumes submitted by an employee get special attention as compared to resumes submitted via the Internet (on job boards, company websites, and mobile apps).

3. Interning (or participation in a Co-op program) is also a very strong way to get an interview and offer for a full-time position upon graduation, particularly if the hiring manager (or a close colleague of the hiring manager) has had a chance to observe your skills and

2

strengths first hand (See the chapters titled *Interning Your Way to a Job and Visa Laws and Your Work Options*).

4. Both volunteering and part-time work, even for a few hours per week on a regular basis, are very good ways to get the attention of a hiring manager or an employee who might bring you to the attention of a hiring manager (or the HR department) for an internship or full-time job after graduation (See the chapter titled *Volunteer or Part-Time Your Way to a Job*).

5. The fifth way that you can get an interview for an internship or full-time job is to impress the recruiter who visits your school during a job fair or an on-campus recruitment visit (See the chapters titled *Taking Advantage of Job Fairs and Mastering Job Interviews*).

6. The sixth way that you can improve your chances of landing an interview requires going around HR by directly contacting the hiring manager—<u>whether or not there is a job posting</u>. HR professionals often follow a relatively slow process, and may not fully understand the skills and strengths desired by the hiring manager. They also may be tied to company policies that discourage the hiring of international students. The hiring manager, on the other hand, is mainly concerned about finding the right candidate as quickly as possible, even if it means bending company policy and procedure. If you engage him directly, and are able to present yourself as an exceptional candidate, there is a good chance that he will arrange for you to be interviewed. As with the first five ways above, this approach will bring your resume priority. **It may be difficult for you to accept the idea that you should avoid the official HR application process, but you will increase your odds of success if you do.**

7. The seventh and least successful path to landing a job interview is submitting your resume online to HR (with or without a cover letter). One reason is that there is a good chance that the hiring manager and HR will find enough candidates using the other approaches already discussed before seriously considering online candidates. Another reason is that the official policy of many companies is to give preference to permanent residents over international students. If you only take the online approach, it can result in a very long and frustrating job search or a job that is less satisfying than one you might have landed if you had used one of the other approaches.

The 3 Steps

"A journey of a thousand miles begins with a single step."

— Lao-tzu, *Chinese philosopher*

"The journey to your job in the USA requires 3 steps."

— Steven Steinfeld

During my years of coaching international student job seekers, I have found them to be especially challenged by the following six factors:

1. Visa Rules and Regulations

2. Communication and Culture

3. Poor Understanding of the Job Search Process

4. Lack of an Established Network

5. Lack of Strategic Networking Skills

6. Poor Job Interviewing Skills

I am about to introduce you to 3 simple steps of DISCOVERY, PREPARATION, and ACTION that will give you the basic structure you will need to follow to overcome these challenges, and separate yourself from your job seeking competitors, including other international students. The successful use of this process requires that you:

- Put your faith in the guidance described in this chapter and throughout this book
- Come to understand the value of your strengths (soft skills) and relationships. Excellent grades and a good technical skill set will not guarantee you a job in the U.S.
- Stay active, positive, confident, and focused.

The 3-Step Job Search Process

Discovery

- Inventory Your Interests, Personality, Personal Strengths (Soft Skills)— Combine with Your Hard Skills, Knowledge, Experience and Goals
- Identify, Research, and Evaluate Jobs, industries and Employers

Preparation

- Develop a Compelling Value Statement, Resume, Cover Letter and LinkedIn Profile
- Create A Written Set Of Goals and a Networking Plan

Action

- Connect with Alumni and Other Potential Influencers at Target Organizations
- Hold Informational Interviews
- Ace the Job Interview

DISCOVERY

Your goal should not only be to find a job quickly, but to find your best possible job at an organization with opportunity for learning, growth,

6

advancement, sponsorship—and a culture where you will be comfortable and productive. The DISCOVERY step explained below will help you to save valuable time by determining which jobs and companies you should pursue.

Even if you think you are on the right path, you should spend a little time validating that path in a Discovery step. There are over 400 broad professional job classifications and over 800 detailed professional job classifications, many of which you have probably not considered. There are also millions of employers in the U.S., including over 18,000 with more than 500 employees, each with a somewhat unique culture.

Even though you may be willing to compromise on a job or company in order to stay in the U.S., landing a job at a company that is an excellent match with your personality, strengths, interests, and work values will put you in the best position to successfully launch your career— and the best position to be considered for sponsorship.

Start by taking an inventory of your strengths, sometimes called "soft skills." These are different from "hard skills" that are training related (e.g. MS Office). Strengths refer to talents that have been developed from a young age and cannot be easily taught. For example, it would be very difficult to train someone to be creative or detail oriented or a great problem solver. As discussed at length in the chapter titled *Mastering Job Interviews*, your unique combination of strengths is often more important than your knowledge, experience or skills in determining whether or not you will be offered the job.

<u>One of the biggest misconceptions international students have is that they believe that they will be judged ONLY on their ability to perform the technical aspects of the job—when it is the candidate with the best combination of hard and soft skills who will typically be offered the job.</u>

Your strengths (soft skills) very likely include several of the following, and maybe some others not listed here:

- Adaptable
- Creative
- High Energy
- Detail Oriented
- Self-Motivated
- Team Player
- Leader
- Planner
- Verbal and/or Written Communicator
- Problem Solver (Critical Thinker)
- Accountable
- Versatile
- Fast Learner
- Results Oriented
- Dependable
- Strategic Thinker
- Disciplined
- Dedicated
- Hard-Working
- Task-Oriented

Your personal strengths (soft skills), along with your interests, and personality and work values, will also determine the companies where you will be most successful. If the position is a good match with your strengths and interests, you are likely to be more engaged in the work and therefore much more likely to do an outstanding job. On the other side, when a job does not work out, it is usually because of a problem fitting into the culture rather than a problem with the work itself. For example, if a team oriented culture is important to you, there is a good chance that you will not be happy or fully engaged at a company that does not particularly value teamwork.

Once you take your strengths, interests, personality and work values into account, add them to your experience, knowledge, and skills—and brainstorm opportunities that are both attractive and realistic.

How to Brainstorm Opportunities

Assemble keywords consisting of job titles and job descriptors into job search engines in various combinations (e.g. "research analyst marketing creative"). Keep in mind that similar jobs often have different job titles. For example, in Vivien's job search, she evaluated postings with a dozen different job titles (market research associate, research analyst, project analyst, web analyst, trading desk associate, assistant analyst, marketing analyst, entry level digital consultant, assistant digital planner, market research intelligence, customer insights analyst, and search specialist).

Use Indeed.com, LinkedIn.com, Glassdoor.com, Vault.com, MyVisaJobs.com and Google Advanced Search for postings and company, industry, career and contact information. You can also try the newer job hunting apps such as Switch and JOBR. Also experiment with career specific job boards (e.g. dice.com for postings of tech jobs, devex.com for international jobs), and with professional organizations and niche websites that you find by using key words in an online search or with the help of your school's career center.

Set up alerts with your keywords on Indeed.com, LinkedIn.com/jobs, and **Google.com/alerts** to automatically be notified of daily job postings that get the best results. Keep the most promising alerts active during your entire job search.

Some job postings that come up will be easy to disregard while others will require analysis. For example, Vivian was very interested in a job posting asking for 3 years of experience. Although she only had 3 short term internships, she was confident that she had everything needed for success as described in the posting. She pursued the job and was granted an interview. As it turned out, the 3 years of experience was a preference rather than a requirement.

How to Evaluate Your Match to a Job Posting

Assess the most interesting job postings by highlighting the job requirements and job responsibilities within the posting in the 3 colors of a traffic light: GREEN, YELLOW, and RED <u>Be sure to highlight every bullet point in the posting.</u>

GREEN: A great fit/This attracts me to the job/I am very confident that I meet the requirement

YELLOW: Does not apply to me/I haven't done this before but I am sure that I can meet the requirement with a minimum amount of training or experience

RED: This is a potential turn-off or deal breaker

You can also mark each Skills related bullet point on the job description with an <u>"H" for "Hard Skills"</u> and an <u>"S" for "Soft Skills."</u> This will give you an idea of the mix of those skills required and preferred by the employer.

Note the relative location of each job requirement, job responsibility, and skill listed. The ones that are most important to the company will be listed near the top of each section.

In general, if you match at least 80% of the requirements in GREEN (with no RED), and also match well with the soft and hard skills near the top of the skills section; the opportunity should be investigated further. If you are really excited about the job, but have a significant education or knowledge gap that makes that opportunity unrealistic right now, you may want to invest in closing that gap so that you can pursue a similar opportunity in the future. You can do this by taking additional classes, pursuing an advanced degree such as a Master's or PhD (with the added benefit that it will give you more time in the U.S. to build your skills, experience and professional network), or by getting hands-on training in an internship or OPT assignment.

If the job is a great fit, but there is one item in red, look for a similar job posting without that one "show stopper." If you see a job that is less than an 80% match, but you are very interested in the organization, check the company's job board for positions that may be a better match. You will sometimes find that you are much more qualified for a job one step below the job advertised.

Once you have selected jobs (and/or industries and companies) to investigate, you will want to set up one or more informational interviews for each one since there is no easier way to assess a job and company culture than by talking to someone who has been working at that job or company. See the chapter titled *The Power of the Informational Interview* for how to arrange and conduct these very important meetings during the Discovery step.

Before leaving the DISCOVERY step, make a preliminary list of jobs, industries, and companies to investigate.

PREPARATION

The second step in your job search is PREPARATION. Start by getting organized with written goals, a contact log, and your calendar. The format and method that you use to get organized does not matter as long as the data is written down. You might use a spreadsheet (sample below) phone app, or even a paper list held by a magnet on your refrigerator.

Company	Internal Contact	Email	Next Contact Date	Contact Method	Goal of Next Contact	Job Position

Next, set your broad job search goals for the next 30 days in the following areas:

- Research:
- Attend:
- Develop:
- Improve:
- Update:
- Set-Up:
- Organize:
- Contact:
- Evaluate:
- Learn:
- Practice:

Once you have your 30 day goals, set goals week by week for no more than two different target positions. Your goals should lead to a variety of activities and approaches including: social networking, phone calls, responses to job postings, networking events (especially those connected to alumni organizations, industry conferences, and professional associations), external recruiters, informational interviews, and engagement with your school's career office. Also include related job search activities such as industry and company research. Your goals should be S-M-A-R-T. This stands for Specific, Measurable, Achievable, Realistic, and Timely.

If you have two (e.g. business analyst and financial analyst), you don't need to spend an equal amount of time on each one. For example, you might spend 80% of your time on activities relevant to your first choice target job, and 20% on activities relevant to your second choice. Of course, some activities (e.g. attending a networking event) might span both your first and second choice targeted jobs. <u>Some weeks will be more successful than others, but each week will be more productive with written goals than without them.</u>

My Job Search Goals	Week of:
First Job Choice: Business Analyst	Second Job Choice: Financial Analyst
To Accomplish This Week	To Accomplish This Week
1- 2- 3-	1- 2- 3-
What I Actually Accomplished	What I Actually Accomplished
1- 2- 3-	1- 2- 3-

At the end of the week, ask yourself the following four questions before setting your goals for the following week:

1. Have I accomplished all of my goals for the week? If not, why not?

2. What's been working?

3. What has not been working?

4. What do I need to do more of? less of? change or improve?

In addition to your written goals, you will need a target prospect log. The following are some of the things you may want to keep track of in this log:

- **Information on your target companies.** Select 10 or 20 companies that hire people like you, then research the company and log the information from your research. This information may include: industry, location, target position, referral contact, the date you submitted your resume and cover letter, opportunity status (e.g.

hot, warm, cold), and additional comments. While identifying and researching target companies, <u>pay special attention to U.S. companies that do business or have locations in your home country or have plans to do business in your home country</u>. You will be networking your way into these target companies whether they have a job posting or not. I will discuss how in future chapters.

<u>Approach all employers who hire people with your talent and potential—except for the relatively few organizations that firmly state a "U.S. Citizen or Permanent Resident Only" policy in their job postings. Be sure to include some established fast growth medium companies and smaller companies known to sponsor international students in addition to the very large companies (especially in technology and business consulting) that are well-known for sponsoring international students.</u> Many employers have not sponsored an international student in the past or may prefer to hire U.S. students, but there is a good chance you will be hired and sponsored if you can impress a hiring manager with your unique blend of skills and strengths during an interview, internship, volunteer or contract assignment.

- **Contact information for people you plan to connect with at target companies.** Include the date that you plan to contact and follow-up with each person, including your method of contact (e.g. email, LinkedIn message).

  In addition to contacts at target companies, you should list and track networking contacts that might be able to provide you with information or advice or introduce you to someone who can provide you with either or both. You might want to keep this contact list separate from your target company list.

  If you are very organized, consider dividing each calendar day into blocks of time for various job search activities. I also recommend that you measure and compare your results each week (new contacts made, contacts added to LinkedIn, number of informational interviews, resume submissions leading to job interviews, and hours spent on each activity). **Spend most of your available time researching companies and potential opportunities, establishing potentially valuable relationships both online and in-person,and setting informational interviews.**

During the Preparation step, you will need to complete an initial value statement, resume, cover letter, and LinkedIn profile. I discuss each of these in some detail in future chapters.

Before leaving the PREPARATION step, ask yourself the following questions:

- Are my job search goals clear and in writing?
- Have I created tools to keep track of my weekly goals and networking plans?
- **Have I developed a compelling value statement, and do I practice it frequently?**
- **Do my resume and LinkedIn profile highlight what I need to get across for the specific jobs I am targeting?**

ACTION

Finally, but not necessarily after a long time, you will enter the ACTION step. In this step, you will concentrate on executing your plan, and also take daily and weekly actions to measure, assess and refine your results.

When you see a job posting of great interest and viability (lots of Green, little Yellow, and no Red), try to quickly locate and meet with an employee (or ally of the hiring manager) who might be willing to bring your resume forward within the company (see the chapter titled *The Power of the Informational Interview* for how to arrange and conduct these meetings).

If you cannot get an informational interview (in person or by Skype or phone) with someone who might be able and willing to deliver your resume to the hiring manager (the person to whom the job reports) within a week or two of seeing the job posting, send your resume with a cover letter directly to the hiring manager. See the chapter titled *Effective Resumes* for tips on how to identify and contact hiring managers and the chapter titled *Compelling Cover Letters for how to write an effective one.*

If you are unsure of the identify of the hiring manager, send your resume with a cover letter addressed to the highest level person whose email address you can obtain (e.g. VP or Director) in the hiring department (e.g. finance, marketing, engineering). If that is also not possible, send your resume and a cover letter directly to the highest level person with a known email address in the HR department (e.g. VP or Director). If there is a specific job posting of for which you qualify, reference it in your email. If not, introduce yourself as someone potentially interested in opportunities at the company. In any case, don't stop trying to set up informational interviews with company employees or allies of the hiring manager who might encourage the hiring manager to interview you.

While in the ACTION step, continually ask yourself the following questions:

- Have I thoroughly identified and researched my target industries, organizations, jobs, and potential hiring managers?
- **Am I bringing quality and professionalism to everything I do? This includes a professional email address and a professional voice mail message on your cell phone.**
- **If I am planning to send my resume and cover letter, have I done everything possible to identify the names, titles and email addresses of hiring or HR managers?**
- **Am I putting enough time into my job search efforts?**
- **Am I using the tools I created to stay organized?**

16

- What do I offer to each job and company I am pursuing? What does each job and company offer me?
- Am I setting myself apart from other candidates?
- What do I need to increase, decrease, improve, or stop doing immediately?
- Do I need professional coaching help? See the chapter titled *Job Search Coaching* to understand the many benefits.

Please note that the ACTION step will often take you back to the PREPARATION step, and maybe even back to the DISCOVERY step.

Before moving on to the rest of the book, please understand that your goal should be to identify and pursue multiple opportunities, but they should all be good ones. Unless you must take a temporary job to meet your financial or visa obligations, do not be tempted by job opportunities for which you are disinterested or overqualified because you are afraid you will not receive a better offer. Accepting such a job can lead to a permanent detour from your intended career path, whether in the U.S. or your home country— and hurt your ability to gain H-1B sponsorship if that is your goal. It can also turn out to be a job where you feel trapped, overworked, underpaid or underutilized. Such a job can have a negative impact on your self-esteem.

If you need to temporarily settle for less than the best job or company, continue to use this book as a guide, and keep working toward better options inside and outside the company. If you find yourself in a very frustrating situation, you should leave as soon as possible, but not before finding a new job. There is no law against quitting a job at any time. An employer will be understanding if you tell him that the job is not working out or that you have a better opportunity, and you offer to give him two weeks' notice prior to leaving.

Developing Your Value Statement

*"Your brand is what people say about you
when you're not in the room."*

— Jeff Bezos, Founder of Amazon

If I gave you 30 seconds to tell me why someone should hire you or why I should help your job search, would you be able to give me a good answer? What if I gave you two minutes?

When someone asks "What do you do?" you should be hearing, "What is your career focus? and "What value can you bring to a particular type of organization?" Respond with a prepared answer while sounding casual and genuine, and include something interesting about yourself to help the other person remember you.

If you are uncomfortable making statements that might sound like bragging, (e.g. "I am great at marketing analytics") instead say, "Both marketing professionals and my marketing professors have told me that I have an exceptional aptitude for marketing analytics." If you have achieved an award in school or at work to support your expertise, you can mention it within your value statement.

Need help getting started? Fill in the form following the example below (if writing in the book, use a pencil with an eraser). Use your value statement while networking in response to a question such as "What do you do?" or "Tell me about yourself."

SAMPLE VALUE STATEMENT

My Career Focus (and at least one memorable fact, preferably related to a strength such as leadership, discipline, competitiveness, or social responsibility)	*I will be receiving a Marketing degree from Steinfeld Business School in May. While in school, I also organized and coached Steinfeld's first table tennis team.*
Highlight strengths, skills, or knowledge that have allowed you to be successful at an internship or job (or at a school, extracurricular, or volunteer project if you have no work history)	*I have a passion for marketing, and already had two successful internships at large media companies. Both marketing professionals and my marketing professors have told me that I have an exceptional aptitude for marketing analytics.*
Explain the work you are pursuing or the types of organizations that are your focus.	*My immediate career goal is to work for a large global company as a Marketing Analyst. I might also be interested in an entry level job as a Digital Marketing consultant, but I don't know much about the consulting industry.*

Ask for informational interview referrals.	*I'm actively expanding my network. If you know people in marketing or consulting who might give me some information or advice, I would very much appreciate their contact information.*

Now practice your value statement. When ready, test it by imagining that you enter an elevator alone with the person who can hire you. You have 30 seconds to deliver your "elevator pitch" before reaching the ground level. Are you comfortable with what you plan to say? Will what you plan to say cause the other person to ask you follow up questions? For example, "At which media companies did you intern, and what did you learn while you were there?" or "How good are you at table tennis?" Speak slowly and clearly when delivering your value statement. 30 seconds is a lot longer than you might think. If you watch a politician give a speech, notice that he uses dramatic pauses in between key words or sentences. You should do the same with your value statement. Give the listener time to reflect on what you are saying.

In many real world situations, your value statement will be delivered after making some "small talk" (See the chapter titled *Strategic Networking*), and you will often not be able to comfortably deliver your entire value statement in one continuous stream. However, if you stay focused, you should be able to get across everything you want to say (and ask) before the conversation ends.

If you can get the other person to talk about himself before you deliver your value statement, it will make it easier for you to decide exactly what to say. For example, if you are interested in a job in marketing, you would choose different words when speaking to a marketing person than you would to someone who knows little or nothing about marketing.

Don't be discouraged by your first attempts to develop and deliver a compelling value statement. It requires practice and continuous improvement.

In addition to the spoken value statement you need for networking and interviewing, you will also want to use modified, sometimes more formal written versions of your value statement at the top of your resume, and within your cover letter and LinkedIn profile. Any time you improve your value statement, update the three written versions. In any event, you should continually refine all four, and tailor each one for different situations and opportunities.

Effective Resumes

*"Excellence is to do a common thing in
an uncommon way."*

– Booker T. Washington, U.S. Educator

This chapter lays out the best advice that I have gathered from career coaching and HR professionals (and have been proven to be successful for my international student job search clients). This does not, however, mean that you should not show your resume to people whose opinions you value, especially people in your field. <u>It is critically important that you see your resume from the point of view of the reader.</u>

When developing your resume, there are four basic points to remember:

1. Easy to read

2. Compelling Summary (or Objective) at the top

3. Relevant

4. Measurable accomplishments

Easy to Read

Take out all unnecessary words, and put yourself into the position of the reader. <u>Is your resume clear and written simply enough for him to get an idea of your potential value in as little as six seconds</u>? This is all the time some readers may take (only looking at your last job title, start and end dates, and education). A hiring manager reading your resume as the result of a personal recommendation may take longer, but probably still less than a minute.

Easy readability is a reason to avoid functional resumes. A functional resume groups your skills and accomplishments to put focus on them rather than on your chronological work history, but makes it hard for the reader to understand when and where your accomplishments were achieved and where and when you used various skills. The same lack of easy readability is true for many "creative" resumes. Requiring more time to be read can result in your resume being trashed without being read at all. You can follow the format in this book, use professional resume templates within Microsoft Office (office.microsoft.com), or utilize resume formats that have been successful for people within your specific field (include getting copies of successful resumes as one of your networking goals).

Compelling Summary at the Top

I am referring to the top of your resume, under your name and contact information. This space is critical since it may be the only part of your resume that may fully capture the attention of the reader.

Right under your name and contact information, you will want to <u>include a summary statement</u> detailing your strengths and accomplishments, although it is not necessary to title that section. To have impact, your summary should contain two to four sentences (or sentence fragments, but not bullet points) explaining the value that you can bring to the job and the organization.

You should not have a completely different resume for each targeted job—particularly since you can only have one LinkedIn profile, and it is likely to be checked by the employer; but you should customize your summary statement for each opportunity to include relevant words or phrases used in the job description. The need for customization is also a reason not to use a resume distribution service, hand them out indiscriminately at job fairs, or post your resume on job boards.

One way to facilitate customization is to put the job posting into a wordle (wordle.net/create) as shown below, and select from the words that are most prominent to include in your summary statement. You can also try jobscan.co.

Many career services professionals suggest that a relatively inexperienced job seeker use an OBJECTIVE (example below) instead of a summary statement on his resume, believing that a summary statement is better suited to the resume of a more experienced professional. Whether you use an OBJECTIVE or summary statement at the top of your resume, the important thing to keep in mind is that employers in a highly competitive job market are much less interested in your career goals than the value you can bring to the company. Be sure to use this space to clearly summarize and communicate your value to the reader. See an example of a well written objective below:

OBJECTIVE

Obtain a summer internship where I can contribute and build upon my excellent knowledge of digital marketing, social media and Advanced Excel, and utilize my interpersonal and problem solving skills.

Relevant

A resume is a marketing instrument, not a biography or legal document. It's critical to get across how you match up with the exact job requirements. Non-relevant information can also make it look like you are not fully in touch with the employer's hiring criteria. An effective resume clearly highlights only relevant work experience, skills, strengths, coursework, awards, activities and accomplishments.

Measurable Accomplishments

Your experience bullets should include measurable accomplishments with action verbs. There are hundreds of possible action verbs that can be used in either present or past tense. Examples include words such as: analyzed, attained, achieved, built, created, coordinated, developed, delivered, evaluated, executed, improved, increased, identified, negotiated, organized, planned, prioritized, produced, recommended, reengineered, reviewed, saved, strengthened, and transformed.

If you find it difficult to think of your accomplishments, try to remember back to times when you have been especially proud of your work on a project at work or school, or when you were praised by your co-workers, supervisors or professors.

Results are usually related to increases in revenue, cost savings, process improvement (e.g. time, accuracy, and quality), and customer or employee satisfaction. <u>If you did not have a direct impact on results, you can talk about how you made a recommendation that helped your employer, department or supervisor meet or exceed a goal.</u> Whenever possible, put a number to the results (e.g. I made a recommendation that helped my department save $10,000).

Don't underestimate your contributions. For example, if you put together an especially effective PowerPoint presentation during an internship that helped the company close a deal, you made a significant contribution to that deal.

Wherever possible, quantify your past results with numbers. These accomplishment bullets should replace statements containing only job duties such as, "Responsible for reorganizing the filing system." Having responsibility for a task like reorganizing the filing system does not say anything about how well you performed; but stating that you "Took the initiative to reorganize the filing of critical documents with a color-coded system that resulted in a 20% savings in access time," says a lot about you. Also, team efforts or results should not be included on your resume (e.g. "Assisted on the company's strategic planning project") unless your personal contribution to the effort is clear.

In Vivian's resume, note that sentence fragments are used, and the word "I" does not appear in the summary statement at the top. Vivian used the same basic resume for all opportunities, but modified her headlines and summaries depending on the job title and job description. <u>I am showing two of her summary statements below that she used to respond to two different opportunities.</u> The rest of her resume remained the same. Please note that the headlines Vivian used above her summaries matched exactly with the job titles in the job postings. Headlines are a good idea if you have room, but they are optional.

Ziya (Vivian) Zhu

ziyavivzhu@steinfeld.edu ♦ 888-888-8888 ♦
www.linkedin.com/in/vivianzhu

ENTRY LEVEL MARKETING ANALYST

Recent business school graduate with strong quantitative and high statistical modeling and data analysis skills, and a passion for marketing analytics. Insight driven reporting and presentation skills, combined with exceptional multitasking, interpersonal, and problem solving capabilities. Fluent in English and Chinese.

Ziya (Vivian) Zhu

ziyavivzhu@steinfeld.edu ♦ 888-888-8888 ♦
www.linkedin.com/in/ziyavivzhu

ENTRY LEVEL DIGITAL MARKETING CONSULTANT

Recent business school graduate with background in digital marketing channels including SEM/SEO, social media, and eCRM. Software skills include Webtrends and Advanced Excel. Exceptional multitasking, interpersonal, and problem solving capabilities. Fluent in English and Chinese.

Once you have developed your headline and summary statement at the top of your resume, place your **EDUCATION** section directly below it. If you have room and feel it is important, you can add a list of **RELEVANT COURSES** to your **EDUCATION** section.

If you are in a highly technical field, you can put a TECHNICAL SKILLS section directly below your EDUCATION section.

Put your work experience in a section titled **PROFESSIONAL EXPERIENCE**. If you have had a particularly relevant or impressive internship, consider listing it first even if it is not in chronological order. All relevant jobs, including part-time, contract, and temporary, belong on your resume. If you have no work history, include a section called **EXPERIENCE**. In this section, put your relevant volunteer work and school projects. Use two to five bullets under each current or past position. You can end each accomplishment bullet with a period or without a period, but be consistent in your use of periods.

Follow **PROFESSIONAL EXPERIENCE** with sections with titles that are most releveant to you. These can include: **ACADEMIC PROJECTS, ADDITIONAL ACHIEVEMENTS** (honors, awards, grants, and scholarships), **EXTRACURRICULAR ACTIVITIES, VOLUNTEER ACTIVITIES, COMMUNITY SERVICE, PROFESSIONAL AFFILIATIONS, ADDITIONAL SKILLS, CERTIFICATIONS, SPECIAL COURSEWORK,** and **TECHNICAL SKILLS.**

The titles of the last section or two can be combined in any way that fits the space available. For example, Vivian combined **ADDITIONAL SKILLS, CERTIFICATIONS, and SPECIAL COURSEWORK into one section on her resume.**

Now look at the remainder of Vivian's sample resume below. Notice that her accomplishments under **PROFESSIONAL EXPERIENCE** are relevant, specific and measurable.

EDUCATION
Steinfeld University, Chicago, IL
Bachelor of Science in Business   May 2016
Major: Marketing, Minor: Psychology
Overall GPA 3.5/4.0

PROFESSIONAL EXPERIENCE

ABC.com, London, England   Summer 2015
Global online cosmetics retailer with 2000 employees and $1B revenue
International Marketing Intern

- Measured the affiliate performance at 50+ women's wear sites by LinkShare, and built relationships with top-20 media publishers; tested email marketing effectiveness in yielding traffic, and proposed to customize content by segments; resulting in 33% increase in promotional sales
- Designed survey questionnaires for 400+ customers and analyzed survey results for Premier Shipping Membership Program; 30% of loyal customers purchased the Membership after the first month
- Developed competitive analysis of 20+ main competitors in China and created shopping guidance and PR materials tailoring to Chinese customers; ABC's comScore ranking increased 400 places after publication

Money Management, Inc., NY, NY   Spring 2015
Marketing & Wealth Management Intern

- Conducted segmented regressive analysis on 300+ clients to create a 3-tier segmentation strategy; result was a 10% increase in the amount of transactions from the "Tier 1" clients after the first two months
- Crafted marketing materials from Money Management internal Advisor Marketing Center and customized the content for five financial advisors

Wireless Lifecycle, Chicago, IL   Summer 2014
Wireless Lifecycle is a global leader in wireless device lifecycle services with 10,000 employees and $8.2B in revenue

Marketing Intern   Summer 2014

- Utilized SPSS and econometric modeling to analyze more than 600 respondents' survey results in a Brand Health Assessment Research project

30

that simplified 40 services into a single, unifying category; leading to a simple and relevant brand positioning statement

- Executed in-depth analysis of Wireless Lifecycle and its five major competitors' social media performance; created visual maps to measure the integration of six social media channels and websites; leading to a brand new integrated social media campaign with 300% increase in followers

EXTRACURRICULAR ACTIVITIES and ACHIEVEMENTS
Business Case Competition Awards, 2015

- BASES Database Marketing Case Competition - 2nd /30 teams; 3rd Annual Conference Case Competition - 2nd/50 teams

Student Marketing Coordinator, Steinfeld University Cinema, 2014

- Created digital marketing campaigns, connected local publications, professors and 11 student clubs to develop Student Marketing Initiatives; gained 2300+likes on Facebook and 900+followers on Twitter, leading to a 20% increase of movie ticket sales

Marketing Coordinator, Europe-China Global Education, 2014

- Developed digital marketing initiatives of this study abroad organization across 50 universities in Europe, and built the partnership with 20+ host companies in Shanghai; 60 students from 12 countries participated in the 2013 Summer program.

ADDITIONAL SKILLS, CERTIFICATIONS AND SPECIAL COURSEWORK

- **Technology:** MS Office 2010, SPSS, LinkShare, comScore, Prezi
- Queens University, Marketing Research, 2016
- **New York College, Innovative Leadership, Spring 2015**

Don't worry about having your resume scanned by a computer through an applicant tracking system (ATS) used by large companies, or waste a lot of time on laborious online applications unless required, such as when applying for a government position. Use your time and effort getting your resume hand-delivered or emailed by an employee or other company influencer to the hiring manager or HR department.

Write your resume yourself, but have your career services advisor, job search coach, or someone else with excellent English grammar skills review and edit it. Work extremely closely with that person to ensure that you are comfortable with every word being used, and it sounds like you wrote it yourself. If you are considering hiring a "resume professional," only do so if absolutely necessary, and only if highly recommended by someone you trust. The fact that someone calls himself a "resume professional" does not mean he is a career or job search coach or that he is competent.

If you are in doubt about the effectiveness of your resume, feel free to send a copy to me for a free review (send to: steven@steinfeldcoaching. com).

Common Resume Questions

Q. How many pages should my resume be?
A. For recent graduates with significant experience and work accomplishments, a two-page resume may be necessary and appropriate. However, a one-page resume is common for a student or recent graduate with a limited work history. If more than one page, be sure to use at least half of the second page or consolidate or reduce information to keep it to one-page. If using two pages, use two separate pieces of paper and put your name and email address in the header on the second page. A longer Curriculum Vitae (CV), which includes a detailed account of academic, public speaking, patents, publications, and research, is required by some legal, scientific, and academic organizations, but is not a factor for most international students in the U.S.

Q. What attributes are employers looking for in an entry level resume?

A. They are looking for relevant knowledge, experience, strengths and skills, a passion for your career, and a record of achievement. They are also looking for a well written document since that will be a good indicator of the professionalism and communication skills you can bring to the organization.

Q. What do you do if your last job was not relevant?

A. Do your best to make the first job listed on your resume relevant to the targeted position. This should be relatively easy if you are a recent graduate, or have had a recent internship, part-time, temporary, contract, or volunteer position that can be made relevant.

Q. Should I include non-work related activities?

A. For recent graduates, non-work activities can help give the reviewer a better overall impression of your abilities. If you were an officer in an on-campus organization, include it to show your leadership potential. Include other activities if they can help reinforce particular strengths. For example, if competitiveness and teamwork are important to the culture of the organization or the job, you might include a mention of your involvement with team sports under **EXTRA-CURRICULAR ACTIVITIES**.

Q. Does volunteer work belong on my resume?

A. Volunteer work should definitely be included on your resume, but it should be made as relevant to the position as possible. Include all your accomplishments as a volunteer under a heading called **VOLUNTEER ACTIVITIES**. If you have no work history, show your volunteer work under **EXPERIENCE** if relevant to the job you are targeting. Please see the chapter titled *Volunteer or Part-Time Your Way to a Job* to understand all the reasons to volunteer during your job search.

Q. How do I identify the name and title of the hiring manager?

A. It's very important to remember that potential weaknesses within your resume, such as lack of experience, may be overlooked if you can get to the hiring manager directly <u>or indirectly with a strong recommendation</u>. You can expect that the hiring manager will always be much more forgiving than his HR professional.

All of the following are ways you can try to identify the hiring manager. Think of yourself as a detective. Continue your detective work until you have all of the names and titles you need.

- LinkedIn. Go to "Advanced People Search" and type in the name of the company and the title you would expect the hiring manager to hold. You can also ask other employees at the company within your LinkedIn network to point you to the hiring manager for the (accounting) job you are interested in within the (finance) department.
- Google Advanced Search. Type in the name of the company and title you would expect the hiring manager to hold.
- Try Hoovers Database or CareerShift.com (if you have access) and/or Jigsaw.com (database is free but may require that you have emails to trade).
- Trade publications such as Crain's Chicago Business (online and print) for the names of executives and professionals on the move or recently promoted.
- Call the company (try the sales department since sales people are usually very accommodating).
- Research the company's website for the names of senior management. If you send an executive an email, you might get a response asking you to send your resume to HR or to him directly, or he might give you the name and contact information for the appropriate hiring manager within the company.

Q. Once I have his name, how do I get the hiring manager's email address?
A. There are several strategies that you can try to get his email address:

34

- Send him a LinkedIn invitation to connect (See the chapter titled *LinkedIn and Other Social Media* for examples of personal messages to include with your invitation). Join as many affiliated LinkedIn Groups as possible since you will have greater success receiving a positive response to your invitation to connect from a fellow group member. Once you are connected, you will have access to his contact information.

- If you have a company contact on LinkedIn, ask your contact if he can give you the email address for the hiring manager.

- Look at the website (and first level contacts at the company if you have any on LinkedIn) for clues on the email convention that the company uses. For example, if you see that other person's email address is steven_steinfeld@abccompany.com, try addressing your email to someone else at his company to firstname_lastname@ abccompany.com. If you send an email, make sure to include your LinkedIn address your signature line so that he can check out your profile.

- Try Hoovers.com, Careershift.com or Jigsaw.com if you have access.

- Call the company. Try the receptionist or sales department. Say that you have some information to send him but do not have his email address. If asked, 'What information?" you can respond with "It's personal."

Q. What do you think of video resumes?

A. While I do not recommend posting your paper resume on job boards other than the one associated with your university, putting a short video version of your resume onto YouTube and your LinkedIn Summary may capture the attention of potential employers. One of the international MBA students I coached at Northern Illinois University, Marion Burette, worked with a friend to develop a video resume (search her name on YouTube to view it). Apart from explaining her education, skills and experience in just over 2 minutes, Marion was able to demonstrate her professionalism, confidence, communication and presentation skills in a way otherwise not be possible.

Q. Should I follow up after sending my resume?
A. Following up is critical, and shows that you care. If you are not following up, you may want to question if you are really interested in the job.

A few days after sending your resume and cover letter to the company, leave a less than 30 second voice message after business hours for the person to whom you sent your resume (remember that you will always be sending your resume to a specific person). You may be able to get to his voice mail box by following the prompts to his name when calling the main listed number, or by asking someone at company for his extension number.

> "Mr Jones, This is Vivien Zhu. I am checking to make sure that you received my resume and cover letter in response to your job posting for an entry level marketing associate. I am very interested in your company, and believe I am a very strong candidate. I can be reached at 888-888-8888. Thank you."

By leaving this message, you will bring attention to your resume, and improve your chances to be called for a job interview. Before you leave the message, practice and time what you are going to say several times. **Speak very S-L-O-W-L-Y and clearly.** If you have a heavy accent or cannot get out of your comfort zone to leave a voice mail, you can deliver a similar message through email.

Additional Resume Tips

- Include your English name or nickname (e.g. Ziyu (Vivian) Zhu)

- Do not include your immigration status (e.g. F-1, OPT, H-1B visa candidate) in your resume since it may hurt your chances to be called for an interview.

- Do not use pronouns in your Objective or Summary or when describing your accomplishments. For example, instead of saying "I developed," just say "Developed."

- Do not include photos, personal information (age, birthday, religion, political performance, self-evaluation, TOEFL score, marital status or references).

- Do not include references or state that "references are available upon request," on your resume.

- Read and reread your resume and then have two other people read it. It will also help if you print out your resume before you review it since you will see errors that you will not spot on a screen. You may get away with one typo or grammatical error, but not two.

- Do not underline, and avoid bold except for headings.

- Use your school email address or a simple Gmail address on your resume for all of your job search correspondence. If you school is well known, you may want to continue to use that address for your job search after you graduate. You can also just use your school's email address for when you contact alumni. Avoid unprofessional sounding email addresses.

- Your home address is optional, but include your LinkedIn address with your email and cell phone information at the top if you have been active on LinkedIn and your profile is up-to-date. If applying for a technical job, you might even consider including a QR code (visibility.com) with a link to your social and professional profiles. If you have an online portfolio, you can include that link at the top as well. Simplify your LinkedIn Public URL under Settings at LinkedIn.com (e.g. linkedin.com/in/vivianzhu).

- If any of your employers are not well known, include a brief description of each company in slightly smaller font under the name of the company. You can easily get a one-line description from its website.

- Do not include skills taken for granted such as MS Office unless knowledge of the most recent MS Office software is important to the job, and avoid older technology references.

- Consider not showing months, except the months associated with your graduation date. Months get in the way of easy reading and sometimes expose gaps that you would rather not show. If you had a job (including contract and temporary) show only the year(s). If you had an internship for a short period of time, use the season and year (e.g. Summer 2016) rather than the months (e.g. June 2016-August 2016).

- Keep careful track of which version of your resume you sent to each recipient on your Contact spreadsheet.

- Include your overall GPA if 3.5 or above. If your overall GPA is less than 3.5, you may want to show the GPA in your major if 3.5 or higher instead of your overall GPA.

- If your major is not relevant to the job, just show your degree.

- Use a simple font like Times New Roman, Calibri or Garamond

- If you have an advanced degree, do not put it next to your name at the top of the resume, such as Yinping (Ping) Huang, MPA, since it may be seen as immodest.

- If you have a paper resume and cover letter, both should be on quality stock such as 24 lb. weight, white or off white linen paper.

- Ask professionals in your field to review your resume in order to help you use language that is particularly relevant in your field.

- Print out your resume to see how it looks before sending it off. Make sure the font is not too small to be easily read or that a one-page resume will not spill over to a second page.

Compelling Cover Letters

"The best way to be boring is to leave nothing out."
— Voltaire, French Enlightenment writer

A cover letter is a document sent with your resume to provide additional information on your skills and experience, and an explanation of why you are interested in the position for which you are applying. It can give you an extra opportunity to build a case for being interviewed, especially if you are a borderline candidate.

Even though a cover letter is not always read, including one is often expected and important since it shows that you are not applying to jobs without a reason or extra effort. However, **I suggest that you NOT include a cover letter if you can't write an effective one.** Like your resume, your cover letter represents your ability to express yourself clearly and effectively in writing. Spelling and grammatical mistakes, or awkward use of language, can severely damage your chance of getting an interview.

Of course, if your resume is handed directly to a hiring manager or HR professional, you won't need a cover letter.

A good cover letter should be simple, easy and quick to read, and relevant—and should not be ordinary and boring such as, "I am applying to the position of Marketing Analyst because I believe that my experience and skills are an excellent match with the job description."

Use no more than three or four short paragraphs, and customize each one.

The first paragraph should include how you heard of the job (from a job posting or referred by someone) and why you are interested. "I am responding to your marketing analyst posting on Indeed.com. My father was a mathematician, and I have been around numbers my whole life, including the time I interned at an investment company while studying for my Masters."

A really good cover letter includes a story, and can even be entertaining. In fact, if you are clever and feel that you need a way to differentiate yourself in your cover letter, make the first sentence an attention-grabber, "Why is a recent Masters in Marketing who grew up playing cricket in India interested in analyzing Super Bowl advertising data?" If you can do this well, your letter is likely to get you to an interview.

The second (and third paragraph if necessary) should state 3 reasons why you believe you are a strong candidate. Include keywords from the job description.

Your cover letter should not be a repeat of your resume, but should either add something new to your resume, "My father is a farmer and I have a highly developed instinct for how your agricultural products should be marketed," or highlight two or three achievements within your resume that are of particular importance but may be overlooked in a quick reading, "I worked at an advertising agency that managed an agricultural account at my first internship, and contributed several innovative ideas to how they measured their marketing campaign."

It is always helpful to mention something that shows you have done your company research. One approach would be to align a company goal or challenge alongside your relevant experience and value such as, "I read in your annual report that your company goal is to increase agricultural product growth by 5% per year. At my last job, I contributed some new ideas to an innovative agriculture related marketing communications program that increased product growth by 15% in a single year.

A second approach would be to align a hiring manager's goal with your relevant experience and value, "In your speech to the National Agriculture Association, you mentioned that developing creative social media marketing programs are becoming critical to success. I recently received Certification in Social Media Marketing from Steinfeld University, and would love to discuss some of the new approaches that we studied with you."

Finish with a short final paragraph that says how you plan to follow up, a final thank you, and your cell phone number:

Notice how the sample cover letter below draws attention to three relevant highlights in Vivian's resume that might be overlooked in a quick reading of her resume.

Hi Mr. Steinfeld,

I'm responding to your Trading Desk Associate posting on Indeed.com. I was attracted to this posting based upon my passion for digital marketing, and the relevant experience that I have gained through multiple internships at multinational firms in different industries. I believe that these experiences fit well with the nine growth factors mentioned in your annual report, particularly the emphasis on globalization.

The following are a few examples of my dedication to building a career in digital marketing:

- I moved to New York for an internship with Money Management, Inc. to build my understanding and skills in digital marketing. During the five-month program, I conducted segmented regressive analysis on 300+ clients to create a 3-tier segmentation strategy.

- I have immersed myself in industry events to learn about emerging marketing technologies, including attending the SES (Search Engine Strategy) conference in NYC.

- My most recent internship with ABC.com, a large cosmetics retailer in UK, gave me the chance to use technology tools to drive insights for effective marketing decisions. When the team needed to assess its publishing partners, I encouraged my manager to use LinkShare to track 50+ publishers' performances, and created Excel models to analyze the data.

I will follow up within a week to confirm that you received my resume, and set up a time to get together to answer any questions you may have about my background. I can be reached at 888-888-8888. Thanks very much for your consideration.

Sincerely,

Vivian Zhu

Cover Letter Tips

- Put your cover letter into the body of your email rather than send it as an attachment.

- Do not sound too formal in your cover letters. Sound confident but friendly. An easy way to do this is to start the cover letter with "Hi" or "Hello."

- Do not attempt to use humor in your cover letter since it may be misunderstood.

- If you use more than two examples, use bullet points to add to the readability.

- Don't say that you are the "perfect candidate" or "the best candidate" since it may sound arrogant rather than confident, and you not likely to be familiar with all of the other candidates.

- Do not attract attention to a competitive weakness, "Although I am not one of the best students in my class in statistics......"

- If you have a strong portfolio, including work or presentation samples, include it as an attachment to your cover letter in addition to attaching your resume

- If you are applying for similar jobs, you can cut and paste some material from one cover letter to another, but customize every cover letter. If you do cut and paste, be sure to proofread the new letter very carefully.

- Remember that your goal is to send your resume and cover letter directly to the hiring manager. If you do wind up sending it to HR, put in the time to get the name of a real person rather than addressing your letter to "Hiring Manager," "Dear Sir," or "To Whom It May Concern." That extra personalization will get your resume and cover letter much more attention.

- Proofread your cover letter very carefully and have a career services advisor, professional job search coach, or friend with excellent English language skills review and edit it.

Strategic Networking

*"I hear and I forget. I see and I remember.
I do and I understand."*

– Confucius

The difference between a disappointing and a successful job search almost always comes down to the ability to network strategically and effectively.

It is very likely that this is not the first time you have been told that you should network, but you may not know exactly why it is critically important to your job search, or how to effectively go about networking with professionals. This chapter will help you overcome your concerns and teach you how to network step by step, even if you are shy or introverted or do not know how to get a conversation started in a new culture.

<u>Job search networking is not about asking for job leads, and it's not about approaching everyone in the same way.</u> Your top networking goal should be to connect with as many people as possible who can give you the information, advice, referrals and recommendations you need to effectively connect with hiring managers and the people who influence them.

I used to tell job seekers that networking contributes to about 60% of professional job offers. Today, I tell them that it's about 90%, and very close to 100% for international students seeking the best jobs and internships.

47

Even so, very few spend enough time networking. In fact, they often spend relatively little time. This is because the idea of networking can appear to be intimidating—even to U.S. students—mainly because networking will require you to sometimes get out of your comfort zone. <u>Getting out of your comfort zone is not easy, but it can be done step by step.</u> It requires courage, but you have already shown that courage by coming thousands of miles to a new country with a very different culture to study and work. Have the courage to ask people for a referral, an informational interview, or a phone call on your behalf—and you will be surprised by how many people are willing (and sometimes eager) to help an international student.

Networking allows you to get to the hiring manager, directly or indirectly, by bypassing HR professionals who automatically eliminate international students from consideration. But even if the company hires international students, your resume and cover letter might not stand out from the hundreds or thousands that may appear to be very similar. Therefore, <u>you should assume that you will not be called for an interview without direct contact with a hiring manager, a personal contact of the hiring manager, or an employee.</u>

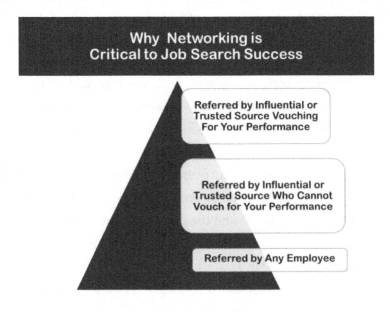

Why Networking is Critical to Job Search Success

Referred by Influential or Trusted Source Vouching For Your Performance

Referred by Influential or Trusted Source Who Cannot Vouch for Your Performance

Referred by Any Employee

On average, 45% of all employees hired in the U.S. are referred to the company by a current employee, and some companies hire up to 80% of their new employees on the basis of a recommendation from a current employee. In addition to employees, interview candidates are often referred by former employees and trusted and influential advisors (friends, colleagues, former colleagues) of hiring managers. <u>Even if a trusted and influential advisor is not directly familiar with your work or strengths, you are almost guaranteed to be referred for an interview if you impress him with what you say in an informational interview.</u> If that same advisor can speak glowingly about your value from personal experience, you have an almost 100% chance of being hired if you do well on your interview.

There is no need to depend on a job posting. You can avoid and eliminate competition if you are introduced to the hiring manager with a strong recommendation before there is a job posting since jobs are always in the process of turning over or being created, and hiring managers would rather avoid the time consuming resume review and interview process if at all possible.

Once the job is posted, company policy may not allow a meeting with the hiring manager until the interview process has been completed. In any case, continue to pursue an informational interview with a company insider who can put in a good word for you as soon as possible (see the chapter titled *The Power of the Informational Interview*). Even if the posted job gets filled before you can get an interview, there is always the chance that a similar job will become available soon.

Now imagine that you and Vivian are both interviewing for a job. You are both qualified, but you are likely to be seen as more qualified than Vivian. Before the interviews start, a trusted advisor to the hiring manager says to the hiring manager, "I understand that you will be interviewing Vivian Zhu tomorrow. I had an informational interview with her the other day. I think she's AWESOME! I'm sure that she would be a great addition to your marketing department. She's passionate about marketing analytics, and has had impressive internships. If I were you, I would grab her before someone else does." Who do you think is going to get the job, you or Vivian?

Plan Networking Activity

Effective networking takes some planning and organization. Start your job search networking plan by mapping your contacts as shown below:

Start Mapping and Prioritizing Your Network	
Friends, Relatives, Neighbors and Spouse/Partner's Network	Current or Former Classmates, Faculty and Alumni
Current or Former Co-workers or Managers	Family Business Connections in U.S.
Volunteer, Community, Religious, Political and Sports Groups or Clubs	Professional Associations or Organizations

Start your job search networking by getting the word out to everyone within your inner circle— and to alumni, former colleagues, and other allies who you feel will be especially supportive. Talking to people in your inner circle is a good way to "warm up" before talking to people with whom you may be less comfortable. You may even be able to have someone in your inner circle, or another ally in your home country, help arrange a meeting for you in the U.S. Also check http://www.internations.org/ to find potentially helpful expats from your country living in the U.S.

Prioritize contacts according to their ability to hire you, connect you with hiring managers and employees at target companies, evaluate your value statement, give you company or industry information, provide valuable career advice or guidance, and/or advocate effectively for you.

When you connect with these contacts:

- Deliver your value statement
- Ask them what they know about organizations on your target list
- Ask for informational interview contacts
- Ask only for information and/or advice

Strategically Expand Your Network

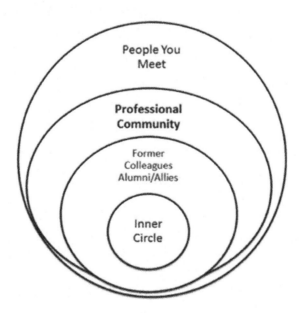

Engage People with Small Talk

<u>Networking in a new culture may be very uncomfortable at first, but it gets easier and easier with a little practice. In any event, you may sometimes need to force yourself to move out of your comfort zone.</u> Start with small talk, which is light, friendly and casual conversation that often takes place while people are waiting or relaxing. Start with practicing small talk with Americans that you meet in the course of your average day, and include something about yourself in the conversation. For example, while you are waiting at the bus stop, you might say to the person next to you, "I wish the bus would get here. I don't want to be late for my next class," or when you pass someone walking a dog, you might say "What a cute dog. What's his name? I'm thinking of getting a dog. Do you think that I could leave one at home alone while I am at school?" A popular topic is the weather, "Beautiful day, don't you think? I wish I didn't have classes today." Once you start the conversation, the other person will often engage with you by asking a question ("It really is beautiful today. By the way, which school do you attend?"). Once that happens, you can move into your value statement.

If you are uncomfortable making small talk, make one of your goals to practice with one stranger every day (e.g. in the supermarket, at the bus stop, while in a queue at the coffee shop). If that's too difficult right now, practice by finding opportunities to make small talk with at least one American friend or classmate each day and slowly move into engaging with strangers.

When engaging with your classmates, take every opportunity offered, including spending time with them at the local pub even if you do not drink alcohol. Not only will it help you to feel more comfortable with U.S. culture, you may get valuable study tips or job leads.

Leverage Networking Events

Even if you are shy or nervous at first, once you are a little more comfortable with small talk, it is important that you attend formal networking events such as career and speaker events at school and professional association meetings or conferences. But you should alos keep in mind that almost any event can be considered a networking event. When you go to a birthday party, go to have fun but also go with the intention to make potentially helpful contacts.

When you go to a formal networking event, whether at your school or elsewhere (try meetup.com, eventbrite.com, techvenue.com, and allconferences.com for events in your industry), you should go with a plan. Your plan should include initiating conversations, tailoring your value statement to each person you meet, and spending between three to five minutes speaking to each individual. This will turn out much better than running around collecting business cards.

Before going to any event, make a short list of potential conversation topics such as recent movies, music, sports, or travel, but avoid topics that may lead to uncomfortable conversation such as religion, sex, money, or politics.

An example of an effective strategy at a networking event would be to wait for people to leave a group or approach people who are standing alone in order to be able to engage one-on-one. Once you do, start by introducing yourself with a big smile, "Hi, I'm Ping Huang." He will respond with his own name. If not a very easy name, ask him to spell it. In any case, remember to use his name several times when addressing him during the conversation so that you won't forget it. Then ask him "Where are you from?" His answer may be a country, state, or city. Tell him where you are from followed by "What do you do?" After he tells you, he will ask you the same question. When he does, deliver your value statement. Before ending the conversation, bring up one of your conversation topics to build some extra rapport before you move on to the next person ("By the way, I just made a date to see the new Disney movie. Have you seen it? What did you think?"). Before leaving, say something like "It was great meeting you." I will send you a LinkedIn invitation when I get home."

Another strategy would be to bring along your extroverted American friend Steven so that he can bring you into a conversation that may prove valuable:

> Steven (speaking to Joe, a corporate Marketing VP): "Joe, I would like you to meet my friend Vivian. She's a recent graduate who's been investigating joining a company in your industry. She has a real passion for digital marketing and is looking for a large global company where she can contribute her skills and continue to build her expertise."

> Joe: "Really? Vivian, your timing is great. I've been looking for recent grads with skills in digital marketing. Please send me your resume."
>
> Steven: "Joe, why don't you and Vivian get together next week? She can bring her resume along and answer any questions you may have about her background".
>
> Joe: "Great idea! Vivian, here's my business card with my company's address and phone number. How about we meet at my office at 3 pm on Tuesday or Wednesday?"
>
> Vivian: "Tuesday is perfect! I'll confirm with you on Monday, and will see you at 3 o'clock on Tuesday. Thank you."

<u>Notice that while Vivian has uttered only 20 words, she has a great interview lined up.</u>

Vivian now leaves as quickly as possible before Joe asks a question that might disqualify her before she gets to their meeting, such as her visa status. If Joe is impressed by Vivian when they meet, he is likely to go out of his way to get his company to hire and maybe sponsor her, but mentioning visa status now may cause him to postpone or cancel the meeting while he investigates and considers his company's sponsorship policy.

Vivian spends time before the meeting researching Joe's company and specifically their marketing programs and investments in digital marketing. She tailors her resume, researches Joe online, and looks for connections on LinkedIn who may be able to give Joe a positive reference about her either before or after their meeting.

On Monday, Vivian sends Joe a simple meeting confirmation email with her cell phone number in case Joe needs to change the day or time of the meeting:

Subj: Meeting Confirmation

Joe, I am confirming the meeting that we arranged for tomorrow at 3p.m. at your office in the Chase Building. I am very much looking forward to seeing you again. In case there is a need for a change in schedule, please contact me on my cell phone at 888-888-8888.

Thank you.

Vivian Zhu

Base Your Networking on GIVING

When you meet new people, look for ways to be a problem solver for them. For example, recommend books and articles, offer connections with people in your LinkedIn network, or tell them about upcoming conferences or meetings. When you do this, others will want to help you in return, and will listen very carefully to your value statement.

Balance Quality and Quantity

One of your goals should be building your contact base by a certain number each week. Whether you network online or in-person, there is almost no such thing as a bad network contact since even the most unlikely person may be able to help move you closer to your goals. Strategic networking requires relationship building, and that requires time and effort. Of all the new contacts you make, concentrate on building relationships with the people who have well developed professional networks in your field, and also show a genuine willingness to assist your job search.

Follow-Through with Gratitude and Reciprocation

It's critical that you follow-through with gratitude after a networking experience. If someone does something for you, return the favor as soon as possible. In all cases, tell them that you are grateful, mention that you intend to reciprocate, and ask if there is something specific that you can do for him now or in the future (e.g. if they plan to visit your home country). If at an event, get his business card and write down the follow-up that you promised him on the back. It's more important for you to get a business card than to give out your own, but you should also have a business card to help others follow-up with you (www.vistaprint.com or a local printer). When designing your card, leave white space on the back for the other person to write something they need to remember in order to follow up.

Keep Your Best Contacts Updated on Your Job Search

Send an email to your best contacts about every six weeks with a piece of information or link to an article that may be of interest to them. End with an update on how your search is going and thank them for the support that they have given to you along the way.

Networking Tips

- Build references starting with your professors and other faculty on campus. Even if you don't get straight A's, you can impress them by your work ethic and commitment to your field of study.

- It's never too late to throw yourself into campus life. There is no better way to practice English and make friends. If there are organizations on campus related to your major, become involved as soon as possible to build networking contacts and references.

- Take advantage of all networking opportunities, including those provided by professional organizations, social networking, and your university.

- Don't worry that you may make a mistake in English grammar or vocabulary. Americans understand that English is your second language, and most will be impressed that you are bi-lingual or multi-lingual.

- Speak slowly and clearly. Look at the person's face to see if they are showing understanding. If not, repeat your message using different words and/or by speaking even more slowly and clearly. Ask your American friends to help you judge if you are speaking slowly and clearly enough.

- Talk to everyone as if they are a friend.

- Look presentable as much as possible during your job search. You never know who you might meet.

- As you arrive at a formal event, remind yourself to give everyone you meet a big SMILE and firm handshake while making direct eye contact.

- Write only your first name on a nametag at an event, and write it BIG.

- Listen carefully to what the other person is saying, and ask for clarification until you understand how you can be of help to him.

- Look for things you have in common with the people you meet, "You love video games? Hey, I love video games!"

- If you don't know something, admit it. People will appreciate your honesty and you will learn something new.

- If you know that certain people are going to a networking event, check their profiles on LinkedIn to get some information that may be helpful in starting conversations.

- Check with your home country's embassy. They sometimes maintain a list of employment contacts.

- Even if you don't attend alumni events, read the alumni newsletter and magazine carefully for networking (and career) opportunities.

- Ask open-ended questions rather than closed-ended ones. For example, rather than say "Did you enjoy your trip to China?" which might get a yes or no answer, say "Tell me about your trip to China."

- Always be reading at least one recently published book. You can use it to make conversation during networking events ("Have you read the latest version of "3 Steps to Your Job in the USA? I have started reading it, and think you would find it helpful"). You can also use it as an excuse to connect with the other person after the event ('If you give me your business card, I will email you a link to the book that I just mentioned, and I will send you an invitation to connect on LinkedIn")

International Student Success Stories

"I've always believed that if you put in the work, the results will come."

– Michael Jordan

My Interview with Vaishali

Vaishali's Background:

Vaishali is now working as a Student/Alumni and Corporate Relations Manager at a major university. Prior to that, she was Career Counselor and Employer Relations Coordinator at another university.

Vaishali originally spent nearly five months dedicated to her job search to find an opportunity that she was truly excited to pursue and that was also an exact match to her skills and competencies. She used all possible work opportunities she could find while at school including volunteering, paid and unpaid internships, and part-time jobs in order to develop and polish the skills necessary to be considered for the career she has now.

Vaishali reveals that informational interviews were her favorite activity within her job search. She conducted over 40 informational interviews within her five month job search with professionals in different industries, roles and cities. She used informational interviews to build her network and gather references in addition to obtaining helpful information and advice. She continues to conduct informational interviews in her current role in order to learn from other professionals as part of her continuing growth and development. During her job search, Vaishali interviewed with 28 employers and got face to face interviews with nine organizations and institutions. She had four job offers before accepting her current role; one that she feels is best aligned with her short and long term goals.

Discovery Step:

Steven: How did you pinpoint jobs to pursue? Did the job that you eventually landed have the same job title or responsibilities that you planned? Were you searching for your dream job, any job, or the best job to launch your career in the U.S.?

Vaishali: Identifying the right job was not the easiest process for me considering that my interests are widespread. Sometimes I wanted to be a part of fast-paced consulting environment, and other times I wanted a much more relaxed environment of general HR office work. But one common theme that ran throughout my process of identifying the right fit was my desire to work with and for people. The people component soon transformed to what is called "Talent" in HR circles, and I decided I wanted to work with individuals in helping them identify the right career direction in a very competitive job market. Fortunately, the job I landed puts me on course for my dream job. During my job search, I felt that it was important to focus on identifying roles and jobs that would eventually lead me to my dream job.

Steven: Did you fully inventory your interests, strengths, and values?

Vaishali: I came to United States with some very diverse prior work experience, and took relevant internships and on-campus jobs that would help lead me to my desired career. I found that it was really important to identify what I gained from each of my past jobs so that I could identify key skills and strengths that made me a better candidate than my competition, and aligned my talent and experience with job requirements.

Before and during my job search I got lots of advice and suggestions on how broad or how narrow my search should be. Is there a right answer? Probably not – It depends! For me, after analyzing and understanding my core interests, strengths and values, I was able to chalk out a plan for myself.

Like most international students. I had a post-graduation time rush. I cannot emphasize the importance of starting early. It's like checking in online early for a flight to ensure that you get a choice seat.

Steven: Did you brainstorm a reasonable number of realistic career and job possibilities?

Vaishali: Owing to my interests and my personality (which makes me believe I could do any job), it was very important for me to identify a reasonable career path and positions of real interest. I used a self-designed 3 point scale of how I rated roles: 1) this one I could kill for, 2) taking a step closer, 3) is a good option. I started working on this a year before graduating and I was surprised how my interests were refined and specific by the time I started applying for jobs, and how many good options I identified.

Preparation Step:

Steven: Were your job search goals, clear, specific, attainable, realistic, and in writing?

Vaishali: I set goals and deadlines for myself. And believe me when I tell you that in the actual job search phase, I felt a lot of pressure. Keeping the right amount of pressure with specific measurable goals, and staying positive, was very critical to my success. What worked for me was giving myself rewards. For example, whenever possible, I took the weekend off from job search when I had a productive week of networking and interviewing.

Steven: Were you organized with weekly goals and a networking log?

Vaishali: I organized my time effectively to make sure I balanced responses to job postings with time networking while in the job search. During the peak of my job search I made it a point to attend one networking event per week or at least 3 per month.

Steven: Did your resume get across what you needed to highlight for the specific jobs you were targeting?

Vaishali: By the time I got a job, I had made more than 200 applications, and I realized that I had customized almost all of my resumes to match the job requirements. It's important for job seekers to understand that their resume may determine if they are called for an interview. The employer should not have to guess if the candidate has the relevant skills to perform successfully in the role. The trick is to make it easy and simple for the recruiter / employer, not make them guess what skills you gained during school or an internship, and how they make you a better candidate than your competition.

Steven: Did you take full advantage of networking opportunities? If so, how? If not, why not? What did you learn most in terms of being prepared for informational interviews?

Vaishali: As cliché it might sound, your chances of getting a job reduce substantially if you don't network. Networking comes naturally to some and not so naturally to others. For most of us (international students), it's all about stepping out of our comfort zone, identifying the right people to talk to and creating a good impression without directly asking for a job or internship. My experience with networking did not lead me directly to a job, but the contacts that I made brought me to several interview opportunities. For any job seeker, it is definitely worth a try. After all, knowing more people can't be bad, can it?

The best way to overcome your anxieties while getting into a conversation with others is making it all about them. I usually begin with 3 or 4 standard questions (e.g. what do they do? where are they from? how long have they been doing what they do?) and other questions that focus all the attention on them. While in a conversation, listen! It's a conversation! Don't treat it like an interview because it is not. When you listen carefully, there will be some points in every conversation you can relate to and that will allow you to take the conversation to the next level.

Action Step:

Steven: Did you make a serious time commitment to your job search? Did you waste time?

Vaishali: Being an international student, most of us come to believe almost immediately that life is going be all good and easy now that I am in US. But believe me when I say that the sooner you get face to face with reality, the happier you will be. I was no different, but I was fortunate enough to have a lot of wonderful people tell me exactly how it was not going to be easy, and encouraged me not to waste too much time if I want to work in the U.S. and maybe settle here.

Steven: Were you proactive enough?

Vaishali: Yes. I was constantly on my job search and doing everything I needed to do. Missing steps or important tasks while in your job search only makes it a longer process. I realized it soon enough that I could not afford to be passive in my job search. It requires a lot of patience and effort to get where you want to go in your career.

Steven: Did you use LinkedIn?

Vaishali: I used LinkedIn as the most important tool to identify people for my informational interviews, networking and also in identifying decision makers at companies where I got an interview. If I were to give any job seeker advice on using social media it would be to let LinkedIn be your Facebook while you're in your job search. All of us (at least I think so) spend a lot of time just randomly browsing pictures and status changes, and seeing what's happening in our friends lives on Facebook. The concept is the same with LinkedIn except you have to be professional in your approach and identify what's important for you to get the best job possible. What really helped me in my journey was setting time aside every day to identify relevant people in strong positions and people who were in a similar situation to my own who might offer me some advice. I sent out lots of notes to people asking for informational interviews, sometimes successfully and sometimes not so successfully. A word of advice; don't take "no" personally, move on!

Steven: Did you make a point of getting to the hiring manager directly?

Vaishali: Yes, every time I applied for a job, I tried using LinkedIn or just made a call to the organization to identify the decision maker for the position. Most people were welcoming in receiving those calls or introductory notes on LinkedIn, but some were not. When they weren't, I didn't let it demotivate me. Finding a job is important, and you should try to do everything you can to get it.

Steven: Did you get out of your comfort zone?

Vaishali: At every stage in my job search there were things I was comfortable doing and there were many other things I wasn't as comfortable doing. I was very comfortable working on developing stellar job applications but I wasn't comfortable reaching out to my contacts to ask for help. When necessary, I got out of my comfort zone, but it wasn't easy.

Steven: What do you think are the keys to a successful job search for international students?

Vaishali: I think that the keys to a successful job search are:

- Meet people and start building relationships early so that you have time to nourish those relationships to the point where they can be fruitful. The U.S. is all about making the right connections. NETWORK!
- Do not take refusals, negative answers and rejections personally. Instead, turn them into motivators, pushing you to try harder.
- While making job applications, spend some time thinking what you would look for in a candidate if you were hiring somebody in the role to which you are applying. It helps you get an employer's perspective. Identify some of the most important challenges the industry or specific organization is facing, and make sure to tell them how you can help them overcome at least one of their challenges.
- Lastly, I would advise all international students who are looking for a job to please not focus on what doesn't work, try to focus your energies on what works for you! If you stay Positive, Persistent and Patient – success will be yours!

My Interview with Vivian

Vivian's Background:

As mentioned in the Preface to this book, Vivian is currently working as an Analytics Supervisor at a global media company based in the U.S.

Discovery Step:

Steven: Did you have a good understanding of your strengths, skills, experience, and work values during your job search?

Vivian: Yes. By working with you, I got to discover that my strength is in quantitative analysis, which is highly valued in marketing analytics and digital marketing positions. Marketing analytics and digital marketing are the areas where my background and passion lie. Also, when editing my resume and LinkedIn profile with you, I reviewed all my past experiences, learned how each one was relevant to my target positions; and the work values that I would bring to the company.

Preparation Step:

Steven: Did you create a format to keep track of your weekly goals and networking contacts?

Vivian: Yes, and I tried to quantify my weekly goals. For instance, one of my weekly goals was to finish five informational interviews with the networking contacts in my target companies. After completing each informational interview, I recorded the information I received, whether or not the contact would be able to refer me, and how I should apply the information s/he provided to my next stage of job search process.

Steven: Did you take full advantage of networking opportunities?

Vivian: Yes. First, networking opportunities are the best way to connect with the insiders who are working in the target company/industry. Second, my interpersonal skills were improved, particularly helpful for leaving a good first impression. Third, networking opportunities helped me get the information about the company/industry. Even when the interviewer was not able to refer me, the information and discussion s/he provided was still valuable.

Steven: What did you learn most in terms of being prepared for interviews?

Vivian:

- Fully understand the job description, and connect "what they need" with "what I have."

- List three key reasons of why they need to hire me, with evidence that I have accomplished those reasons in my past experiences.
- Strategy is important, but practice is the key.

Action Step:

Steven: Did you waste time during your job search? How? Why?
Vivian: No. I learned from everything I did. And it was always good to practice interview skills even when I didn't get the job in the end.

Steven: Did you get out of your comfort zone? When and how?
Vivian: Yes. I reached out to network contacts that I had not met in person on LinkedIn for informational interviews. Some of them actually became my close friends in the end, and we still keep in touch and hang out together in the city.

Steven: What are the keys to a successful job search?
Vivian:
- Know yourself (your strengths, skills, and values)
- Know your target organizations (their goals and challenges and what they value in their employees)
- Learn and practice job search skills (e.g. value statement, interviewing)
- The very best advice I have for other international students is: do your research, network, and always keep a positive attitude

My Interview with Wen

Wen's Background: Wen came to the U.S. from China with a Bachelor's Degree in chemical engineering from China, and earned a Master's in Chemical Engineering at the Illinois Institute of Technology. Despite the fact that chemical engineers are highly sought after in the U.S., and she was highly qualified, Wen submitted several hundred resumes to potential employers with few responses because she was not fully aware of the strategies and tactics described in this book at that time. Four months after graduation, she finally landed a job as a R&D Formulation Scientist at a skin care company. Wen was lucky that the company read her resume carefully and recognized that she had the unique skills necessary to fill an open position for which she did not apply—a very rare event! I am including her interview, because in the end, she learned some valuable lessons.

Discovery:

Steven: Did you fully inventory your interests, strengths, and values?
Wen: I didn't consider my interests, but I thought deeply about my strengths and the value I can bring to a company. I read hundreds of job descriptions on job search boards to figure out which jobs matched well with my skills and experience. One thing that I learned is that **I should have prepared for job searching sooner.**

Preparation:

Steven: Did your resume get across what you needed to highlight for the specific jobs you were targeting?
Wen: Yes, I highlighted my internship and research assistant experience. I also highlighted my research skills, and my patent (for a new pen refill, National Utility Model Patent of China X) which shows that I am innovative.

Action:

Steven: Did you make a serious time commitment to your job search? Did you waste time?
Wen: I gave myself six months to look for a job. If I couldn't find one during those six months, I planned to go back to my country. While I wasted

some time, I almost always followed a schedule of sending 10 resumes per day, 5 days per week.

Steven: Were you proactive enough?

Wen: I regret that I should have done more than just apply to jobs on Internet job boards. For example, I should have attended more professional networking meetings and contacted companies more directly.

Steven: Did you use LinkedIn?

Wen: Yes. It is a useful tool. I could build my own network by connecting to recruiters, schoolmates, and people of my same nationality. Because recruiters have more job openings than they post online, I felt that I might get an opportunity if I connected to them, and they saw my profile. Some recruiters actually did contact me, although few jobs were for international students.

Steven: How did you finally land your current job?

Wen: I applied for a job that I didn't get, but the company contacted me to interview for another job that they felt was a better fit with my resume. I had a phone interview and on-site interview and was offered the job three days later. I am currently working under OPT, but the company plans to sponsor me for an H-1B visa.

Steven: What do you think are the keys to a successful job search for international students?

Wen:

- Stay hopeful!
- Know your competitive advantages.
- Understand the value of your experiences and skills.
- Beyond your work skills, impress the interviewer with your personality and communication skills.

Wenwei's Story

Wenwei was a student in the MBA program that I coached. I stayed in touch with her after graduation and helped her job search with advice when asked. As this book was going to press, I asked her to write about her experience landing a job in the U.S. since there are many lessons to be learned from her experience. Her story is below, followed by what I feel are Lessons Learned that I hope you take into consideration when starting your search.

Wenwei: Like my Chinese classmates, I applied for OPT one month before I graduated from the MBA program. Since I started my job search late, I applied for at least 30 positions online every day, mostly in accounting and finance, but I was consistently rejected. After a few months, I went to the October Job fair where I spoke directly to company representatives. I applied online to 20 companies who were at the fair and two resulted in interviews. After being rejected for these jobs, I realized that I was not applying for jobs that were the best match with my education, knowledge, personality and skills. I decided to pursue a position in marketing, but I was only offered interviews for sales jobs of little interest such as selling Direct TV at Sam's Club. At that point, I made up my mind to give up my OPT and move back to China. Before I left the country, I went to a Tiffany jewelry store to buy a gift for my mom. While shopping, a Tiffany sales person mentioned that Tiffany was hiring Chinese speakers for seasonal Christmas time sales positions. I applied online immediately after leaving the store, completed a 75-minute online test, uploaded my resume, and was contacted to arrange an in in-person interview the very same day. I contacted Steven Steinfeld for help with my interview skills, and was more confident after a mock interview with him. The interview turned out to be a pleasant and successful experience that lasted an hour. I never thought I would work in a retail store for a luxury brand, but I was very excited to get an offer of employment even though it was only a temporary holiday season position. After working at Tiffany through the holidays, my supervisor tried to get me a long term position at the corporate offices. It did not work out, but my job in sales was extended beyond the holiday season.

While I was working at Tiffany, I moved to an apartment near the store and spent most of my free time at the mall where Tiffany is located. Since I play the piano, I was attracted to the Steinway & Sons store where they allow customers to play their pianos. One day, the manager and I started chatting. Over the next 20 minutes, I told him about my education and my job at Tiffany. At the end of our conversation, he told me he thought I would be a great sales representative candidate for Steinway & Sons, and he asked me whether I would like to meet the Regional Sales Manager. When I arrived home, I sent the store manager a thank you note and LinkedIn invitation.

A short time later, I received a phone call from the Regional Sales Manager. The talk was short, and while it seemed like an informal conversation, she asked me some in-terview type questions about my background and career goals. Since the Regional Manager was unsure where I might fit into her company, she invited me to help at an upcoming Chinese New Year piano promotion where she could get to know me better. A week later, I met her at the event at the piano gallery. While there, I met a Tai-wanese friend of the Regional Sales Manager. Networking with her led me to my cur-rent OPT job since she referred me, with a strong recommendation, to a friend who owns a mortgage company. I am currently working there as a Mortgage Associate, but since they are unlikely to sponsor me, I am continuing my job search.

Lessons Learned:

- Applying online alone is usually not successful
- Skipping the Discovery step leads to wasting valuable time

- Starting a job search late limits your opportunities
- It's important to get coaching help when you are not confident of your job search skills such as networking or interviewing
- Networking (sometimes in unexpected or informal settings) is the key to success
- A temporary position can lead to a long term opportunity
- Don't give up! Persistence is often the determining factor

LinkedIn and Other Social Media

"Social media allows me to pick my times for social interaction."

– Guy Kawasaki, Silicon Valley Entrepreneur

Did you know that more than 80% of employers will post jobs and check profiles on social media—mostly on LinkedIn—and 3M job seekers per month credit social media with helping their job search?

While Twitter and Facebook and other social networking sites (including your home country's social media sites) can be helpful to your job search if approached and managed strategically and professionally—**LINKEDIN IS YOUR BEST AND MOST NECESSARY RESOURCE.**

LinkedIn is a worldwide electronic networking tool created specifically for professionals to help in researching people and companies, industry trends, and relevant business topics. The more active you are on LinkedIn, the better you can tell your story, establish your credibility, develop your reputation, and make valuable connections.

There are at least a dozen reasons to actively use LinkedIn:

1. Your LinkedIn profile is much more than your online resume. More than 90% of employers will check profiles on social media—mostly on LinkedIn.

2. On LinkedIn's built-in job board, you can search by job title or keywords, job function, industry, and experience level. You can also search by company name and location, and set your job search preferences. LinkedIn will also make recommendations for you and allow you to set up alerts that will keep you posted by email to new job opportunities that may be a good fit for you.

3. Allows you to engage in "passive search." Employers scan LinkedIn all day long, using keywords looking for candidates with specific skills and knowledge to fill their jobs.

4. Helps you identify target companies that hire candidates with your skills and background.

5. Provides a door opener to face-to-face networking with employees at target companies that can lead you to informational and job interviews.

6. Prepares you for informational and job interviews by researching employers and interviewers.

7. Allows you to request introductions to senior professionals you would not approach on your own.

8. Helps you stay in touch with mentors and university faculty, and former classmates and influential alumni who can recommend you for interviews where they are working.

9. Allows you to easily find and exchange information with professionals, including recent graduates, in your field.

10. Demonstrates your interpersonal, networking, collaboration and social media skills. Many companies search candidates' LinkedIn and other social-media accounts to get a better feel for a candidate's personality and to judge how well he communicates.

11. Allows professionals and recruiters to screen you before agreeing to provide you with information, advice or interview opportunities.

12. Creates a global presence online. In most cases, your LinkedIn profile will be near or at the top of a Google search of your name, and your "searchability" (ability to be found online) will also be increased by your use of keywords throughout your profile.

If you are new to LinkedIn, know that getting started is easy, and there are many LinkedIn tutorials online (Google search "LinkedIn tutorials") in addition to the instructions given on LinkedIn. Once you are comfortable with the basics, add the tips below to enhance your LinkedIn experience and improve your results.

My 15 Favorite LinkedIn Tips

Please note that while individual LinkedIn features are always subject to change, your objectives should remain the same.

1. **Develop a Strong Headline and Summary**

   Pay special attention to your Headline as this will be the first piece of content about you that will be read. Your headline is the area directly under your name. Edit your headline to allow people visiting your profile to immediately understand who you are and where you want to go in your career. Add any important skills that you are developing or have already been developed. For example:

"Recent Business School Graduate with Expertise in Marketing Analytics and Digital Marketing | Fluent in English and Chinese"

---

2. Complete Your Profile to 100%

Completing your profile will make you much more successful on LinkedIn, especially since you will be more likely to be found by employers. Having a complete LinkedIn profile is especially important to an international student who has relatively few connections. If you have relatively few connections AND your profile is not complete, it may send the message that you are not active on LinkedIn. LinkedIn will help you by measuring the completeness of your profile and offering suggestions if necessary on how to complete it and make it stronger.

3. Pay Special Attention to Your Profile Photo

Your photo is the first thing people are going to look at when they visit your profile. Not having a photo, will make a visitor to your profile wonder if you are serious about LinkedIn and/or ashamed of your appearance. Most importantly, if there is no photo, they may not feel comfortable connecting with you. Use a professional looking headshot, but you do not necessarily need to use a professional photographer. Check out my former intern's photo below as an example to follow.

Cici (Shiyue) Chen 1st

Master Student Majoring in Human Resources Management | Talent Acquisition | Compensation | Social Media

Greater Chicago Area | Human Resources

Current	DePaul University
Previous	United Airlines, Career Transitions Center of Chicago, International Student USA
Education	DePaul University

Send a message ▼

192
connections

46

4. **Match Your Profile to Your Resume**

    Your resume should speak to your target audience. Since you cannot have multiple profiles on LinkedIn (a good reason not to be developing several completely different resumes for different opportunities), your profile should match the most preferred and realistic opportunity you are targeting. All experiences and dates on your resume and LinkedIn profile need to match.

5. **Go Beyond Matching Your Resume**

    Instead of cutting and pasting, edit the information and add additional detail to your responsibilities and accomplishments. LinkedIn gives you the option to add media samples to the Summary, Education, and Experience sections on your profile as well as adding additional information (e.g. Languages, Publications, Honors & Awards, Certifications, Projects, Test Scores). It will be helpful to use one or more of these opportunities to differentiate your profile from other international students. Keep in mind that your LinkedIn profile should make people viewing your profile not only want to connect with you—but ultimately refer, recommend, or hire you.

6. **Bring Your Profile to the Top of Search Results**

    Since recruiters are constantly searching LinkedIn for candidates using keywords and job titles, you will want your profile to appear as high as possible in the results of those searches.

    After you have completed your profile to the 100% level, go to "Advanced People Search."

    Enter keywords that describe your targeted position.

    Enter your location.

Hit "Search." Does your profile appear on one of the first few pages of results?

Now open the profile of the person that appeared at top of the first page of the search results. The keywords that LinkedIn used to filter the search will be highlighted.

Repeat the search using job titles instead of keywords.

Now go to your own profile and increase the use of the most important keywords and job titles that you believe recruiters at your targeted jobs would most likely use when scanning LinkedIn for candidates. Note that the more specific you make your keywords and job titles, and the more times they appear, the higher your position will be in a LinkedIn search.

7. **Get LinkedIn Recommendations**

    It is very helpful to get at least three and up to ten strong recommendations from your former managers and co-workers at your most recent jobs and/or your professors to highlight your strengths and show that you were a valued employee and/or student. Make sure that you give your recommenders ideas on specific attributes or accomplishments they might include in your recommendation, but don't write it for them unless they ask you to do so.

    You can also collect Endorsements under the Skills heading by asking your trusted connections to endorse your skills in a LinkedIn message ("Steven, I would appreciate it if you would endorse a few of my top skills. It only takes a few seconds. Thanks very much."). If just a few people endorse you for a specific skill, it won't matter much, but if 20 or 30 people endorse you for that skill, it can be meaningful to a potential hiring manager. This is why it is a good idea to show your top 10 skills in priority order while pushing down other skills that people may add that do not fit well with the brand you are trying to create.

Generally, the more Recommendations and Endorsements you give, the more you will receive. While I do not suggest that you give an insincere Recommendation or Endorsement just to get one, when you request a Recommendation, I encourage you to consider offering to write a Recommendation in return.

If given the option between receiving a Recommendation or an Endorsement, always choose the Recommendation. You will always have a chance to review and approve every Recommendation before it is posted as well as delete ones that no longer fit your target jobs.

8. **Customize Your Invitations**

It is common and acceptable to send an invitation to connect to a professional you do not know without an introduction—but do not send the standard generic invitation, "I would like to add you to my professional network on LinkedIn." It is good professional practice and etiquette to send a personal LinkedIn message reminding the contact how you met or where you worked or went to school together, or something or someone you have in common. Don't hesitate to appeal to his ego. For example, you might send the following invitation:

"Professor Steinfeld, You may remember that I was in your Business 101 class a few years ago. I am expanding my LinkedIn network to include some of our university's most admired professors. I would be happy and honored to share my network with you."

In order to get this personalization option, you must click on the "Connect" link on the person's actual profile.

Avoid clicking the 'Connect' button from anywhere else other than the person's profile, since this will automatically send out the generic invitation. Also avoid sending a broadcast invitation to multiple people since you won't be able to personalize each one. Start with people in your inner circle plus your current and former classmates and co-workers, and expand from there. Before sending invitations, read through each person's profile. You may pick up hints on specific ways you can offer to assist them immediately that you can include in your message. If you don't know them very well, you may want to remind them who you are, who you have in common, and let them know why you think it might be mutually beneficial to connect with them. Don't mention your job search within your invitation. You will do this in a follow-up email or LinkedIn message.

Don't worry if people don't respond immediately. Some will respond quickly and some slowly, and some may never respond; but that's one of the things that will help you determine your most promising LinkedIn relationships.

9. **Use "Advanced Search"**

Use "Advanced People Search" to find network contacts working at your target companies. Look particularly for employees who graduated from your school with a similar degree and/or came from your home country.

Also use "Advanced People Search" to find people who worked at your target companies in the past and where they have gone after leaving the company. You can use this information to help broaden your list of prospective employers within a specific industry, and you may be able to find some informational interview contacts who can give you honest feedback about companies on your target list.

When you find people who have recently joined your target company, make an attempt to get LinkedIn with them and send them a request for an informational interview, "I have been researching opportunities at your company and noticed that you recently joined. Can we spend a few minutes together in person or on the phone so that I can understand why you joined the company?"

10. Identify and Follow Target Companies

Put keywords and/or industries into the search box under Companies (e.g. "finance analyst manufacturing"). Filter the results by geography. Add companies of interest to your targeted company list. Follow them for company and career information, news, and new job announcements, and look for any 1st and 2nd degree connections who work there or recently worked there. It is also possible that the company will check its Followers to look for job candidates.

11. Benefit from Joining LinkedIn Groups

Join groups that contain people who work in your target industry and companies, but who are not currently connected to you. Participating in friendly and informative groups on a regular basis is a relatively easy way to identify potential new contacts that will be more likely to accept an invitation to connect, while also building credibility in your field.

There are hundreds of thousands of groups to join on LinkedIn (with thousands more started each week), but they require permission from the group leader before your membership becomes active. Select groups that reflect your interests, area of expertise, industry, alumni, passions, social causes, and other aspects of your identity. Start by joining your college and or/graduate school alumni groups, and local industry groups in cities where you may want to work when you graduate. Feel free to join a large number of groups including my group, **Steinfeld International Student University, Internship & Job Search News.**

12. Customize Your Profile URL

Customize your profile URL so that it's not a long list of letters and numbers. Click on "Settings" (under your name) and go to "Edit Your Public Profile," and simplify your LinkedIn domain name under "Customize My URL." An example would be www.linkedin.com/in/stevensteinfeld. Once customized, add it to the top of your resume and the bottom of your emails.

13. Use the LinkedIn Job Board

When you access a job within the "Jobs" tab, LinkedIn will immediately show the connections in your network who work for the company. Save the keyword searches that give you the best results, and set them up to alert you to new job postings by email. Each job posting will also offer links to similar jobs and to the jobs that viewers of the job you are looking at also viewed. These are great ways to uncover additional opportunities of interest without much effort. Some jobs will allow you to apply on the LinkedIn site or route you to another site where you can being the application process. **Avoid this temptation!** Instead, find people who work in your field within the company, send them a LinkedIn invitation followed by an email asking them to share information and advice with you in person or by Skype or phone. This will lead to important additional company information and advice from someone within the company and often leads directly or indirectly to an internship or job interview.

14. Take Every Opportunity to Connect

You never know who might be connected to someone who might help you be successful. Since most professionals are LinkedIn users, it's a good idea to ask almost anyone you engage in conversation if you can connect with them on LinkedIn. If you ask them to connect with you, they may forget, so it is best to send invitations to them.

As an international student, you have little to lose by accepting all invitations to connect except for those that seem suspicious (e.g. not from someone in U.S. or your home country and no reason given for the invitation).

One of the techniques that I recommend to my clients is to keep track of the people who are viewing your profile. Unless you are a Premium Member, you will be able to see only a very limited number of people (e.g. five) that viewed your profile. Take the opportunity to view their profile. Look at their background and experience, and the groups that they have joined.

If in doubt as to why the person contacted you, accept the invitation and then send the person a message saying, "I am happy to share my network with you, but curious to know if there is a particular reason why you asked to connect with me at this time."

Consider inviting me to join your network (www.linkedin.com/in/stevensteinfeld) to greatly increase your number of second level connections. I have thousands of connections and my profile is in the top 1% of all LinkedIn profiles viewed. I will immediately accept your invitation if you mention that you are a reader of this book.

15. Take a Look at Job Seeker Premium Status

For many international students, it will be unnecessary to upgrade to paid status on LinkedIn. However, you might consider a paid upgrade if you feel that the benefits offered (e.g. InMail messages, expanded information on job postings and profile views, premium profile and keyword suggestions) are worth the investment. One of the best new Premium features is Open Profile Messages which are free InMail messages that can be sent to any member with Open Profile turned on, even if they are outside of your network. Go to http://premium.linkedin.com/jobsearch for current features and pricing. LinkedIn offers the ability to sign up for a month by month subscription that you can cancel if you feel that you are not getting a good return on investment, and often offers a 30 day free trial.

Social Media Tips

- Start by doing a Google search on yourself to see what comes up. For one thing, you will see what potential employers may see. If there is something you do not want an employer to see, you will not be able to delete it unless you contact the webmaster of the specific page. If you are able to get more recent and positive listings, they will push less positive listings lower down in a Google search.

- Employers often check Facebook accounts to get an idea of their job candidate's character. Even if you have nothing to hide, some postings may reflect poorly on you. To be safe, limit your posts to only your close friends. If you are concerned about things that might embarrass you if seen by a prospective employer, go through your timeline and delete those posts.

- Always keep a positive attitude and ensure proper English grammar on LinkedIn and your other social networking sites.

- Use the same professional LinkedIn photo, and the exact same name, for all of your social networking sites, including Facebook, while job hunting.

- Utilize Twitter to create opportunities for informational interviews by interacting with people connected to your target industry. It is also a good way to stay tuned into target companies, some of which tweet new job postings. Start with a professional-sounding bio under 140-characters since the rest of a longer bio will not be immediately visible. Go to hashtags.org to find Twitter feeds that may be helpful, and to find out when they are most active.

- Post diverse content to drive traffic to your social media sites such as questions, insights, recommendations, and links to articles of interest, videos, or books.

- If you have an impressive work portfolio, put it on LinkedIn, a personal website, pinterest.com and/or one of the online platforms available for that express purpose.

- If you are pursuing a job where social media or networking activity or expertise is important, an employer may ask you for your Klout score. Get to understand Klout and check your score at Klout.com. In addition to Klout, you can source news and insights specific to your field to share online and discuss during your in-person networking activities by using apps such as Scoopit.com or Pulse (a LinkedIn application).

- Consider making a video resume (see the last paragraph of the chapter titled *Effective Resumes*) to add to your LinkedIn profile, blog and other social media sites.

Taking Advantage of Job Fairs

"Luck is what happens when preparation meets opportunity."

— Seneca, Roman philosopher and statesman

A job fair (also commonly referred to as a career fair or career expo) is an event where employers, recruiters and schools meet with prospective job seekers. Even if you are a first year student and the first job fair of the year is scheduled shortly after the beginning of classes, plan to attend. Even if you are not ready to take full advantage of the benefits, you will gain valuable experience for the next fair.

Before the Fair

Update your resume and have it reviewed by a career services advisor well in advance of the fair.

Get a list of companies coming to the fair, and research ones of particular interest before you go, practice your value statement, and prepare some questions that you will want answered such as "What is the standard

89

hiring process?" or "What does your company look for in a candidate?" In addition, you will want to remember to ask for the name of the relevant hiring manager.

A job fair can also be looked as providing mini-interview opportunities, so prepare to answer the same basic questions you might be asked at a job interview (see the sample questions in the chapter titled *Mastering Job Interviews*).

At the Fair

To stand out, engage company representatives in conversation and ask them for their business cards. This will allow you to connect with them by email and LinkedIn after the fair.

Leave resumes with employers only if you feel that your resume does not need to be customized to the company or position. An exception would be when asked by the company representative while speaking with him. In that case, deliver your value statement, hand him your resume (even if not customized), and ask him to arrange a job interview.

In addition to engaging with employers, also use your time at the fair to network with other students who may have uncovered useful employer information.

After the Fair

Whether or not you left a copy of your resume with the company, send a copy (updated if necessary) attached to a note such as the one below a few days after the fair. You can send it to the company representative you met at the fair or the hiring manager if you have his contact information.

Subj: Steinfeld University Job Fair

Dear Mr. Jones,

I was impressed with what I learned about your company at the Steinfeld University career fair, and in my research after the fair. I would appreciate a brief meeting to introduce myself and learn more about potential opportunities at your company. I am graduating with a degree in Marketing in May, and believe that I can make a contribution to the development of your social media program.

My updated resume is attached.

I will follow up with you next week. In the interim, I can be reached at 888-888-8888.

Thank you for your consideration.

Sincerely,

Vivian Zhu

Job Fair Tips

- If you feel the need to have your resume reviewed by a career center advisor prior to the fair, do not wait until the week of the job fair since the career office will be extremely busy that week.

- Bring notes from your company research and a list of at least 3 questions to ask each representative.

- Dress professionally.

- Bring more resumes than you think you will need.

- If you plan to approach companies for two different positions, you can bring two sets of resumes with different summary statements, but you will need to carefully log which resume you gave to which company representative.

- Get maximum time with company representatives by being one of the first students to arrive.

- Get a copy of the program and list the companies you plan to approach, but stay open to adding companies that are not on your list.

- Practice your approach with companies of less interest before engaging your "top" companies.

- Do not ask if the company sponsors international students for H-1B visas, or about salary and benefits.

- If you engage in conversation with the representative of a company you have not researched, tell the representative that his company is one that you have not researched, and ask him if he has time to give you some background on his company at or after the fair.

- Start and end your conversation with the company representative with a friendly smile, a firm handshake, direct eye contact, energy, and a confident posture with your shoulders back.

- Make sure you take each representative's business card and company literature.

- Take notes on how to follow up on a small pad or your phone right after leaving each conversation.

- Go to job fairs at other schools and venues in your area in addition to your own. Find them at www.nationalcareerfairs.com.

The Power of the Informational Interview

"You Create Your Opportunities By Asking
For Them."

– Shakti Gawain, New Age Author

An informational interview is a meeting in which a job seeker asks for first-hand career, industry and company information and/or advice rather than ask about job leads or job openings. Informational interviews have made the difference for almost all of my international student clients, and it's where you want your networking to take you. **Scheduling and holding in-person informational interviews should be at or near the top of your weekly goals.**

Always keep in mind that an informational interview should be handled in the same professional way you handle a job interview, but should be treated more as a conversation than a question and answer session.

Sometimes an informational interview will lead directly to a job offer with little or no competition, but this should not be your expectation or your only reason to pursue these interviews. There are many other important benefits to holding these interviews during both the Discovery and Action steps of your job search.

Informational Interview Benefits (Discovery Step)

- Understand the ideal skills, strengths, knowledge, education, experience, and credentials or certifications required for specific jobs. The answers will help you validate if a company, job or industry that you are targeting is an excellent fit for you.

- Expand your job market and industry information. What are the current challenges and goals within the industry? How does that align with what you offer? In the course of the meeting, you may also come to know that there is an excellent job market for your targeted position, or you might find out just the opposite.

- Discover relevant job titles. Often the same job has different titles at different companies. Learning as many as possible will help you expand your use of key words in online searches, and may help guide your choice of what to use as your resume and LinkedIn profile.

- Find out about jobs and career paths you have not considered or didn't know existed. ("Ping, I know that you are looking at research analyst positions, but have you looked into becoming a data scientist? I think you would be great and you would have a better chance to get a job at my company.")

- Practice your value statement and C.A.R. (Challenge, Action, Result) stories (see the chapter titled *Mastering Job Interviews* for a full explanation of C.A.R.), and talk candidly about your career goals to test the reaction.

- Get resume advice from someone in your field with a successful resume.

Informational Interview Benefits (Action Step)

- Gain first-hand information about company goals, challenges, and immediate needs. This will help you tailor your resume and formulate your questions and answers for a potential job interview. You may also find that there is a company reorganization or expansion coming soon, or that former international students in your targeted job are leaving for good reasons. Such information can be of value to you in deciding if and when to pursue a job interview.

- Meet potential recommenders and hiring managers. The person sitting across from you on an informational interview may be your next boss or mentor - or the influential colleague who can introduce you with a recommendation to the hiring manager.

- Understand the culture of the organization. The informational interview is a great way to identify a potential mismatch before you spend more time pursuing a job at that company with an unacceptable culture.

- Build confidence for job interviews. The more positive feedback, and the more you practice interviewing, the more your confidence will grow.

- Understand if you are connecting. You will quickly grow to understand when you are not connecting. If you are not connecting, you will know that you need to make adjustments in your communication style, answers, value statement, and/or your appearance. You will know you are not connecting if there is no offer of follow-up help.

- Expand your network by asking for referrals to at least two other professionals at the end of each informational interview.

Q. Who should I target for an informational interview?

A. Theoretically, the best target is the hiring manager, but you are more likely to be more successful targeting employees who report to him. Sometimes the person who gives you the informational interview will give you information and advice, but will not be willing to bring your resume forward. However, if you can keep getting referrals from employee to employee, you are likely to eventually connect with someone who will be willing to bring your resume to the attention of the hiring manager (or HR).

Start with a simple connection request on LinkedIn (see an example later in this chapter). Focus on alumni from your own undergraduate and/or graduate college or university, and then move on to others with whom you have something in common starting with employees from your home country. Be sure to schedule some informational interviews with successful recent international student grads in your same field to understand how they landed their jobs and to learn about potential opportunities at their companies.

Q. What questions should I ask during the informational interview?
A. Spend the first few minutes of the interview asking the person you are interviewing about his own experience with the company (e.g. how he was hired, his career prior to coming to company, outside interests, family, and if he has visited or is interested in visiting your home country). People love to talk about themselves. In fact, the more you allow people to talk, the more they will think that it was a wonderful conversation. Mention or comment on anything that comes up that you have in common in order to strengthen your connection and improve your chances for being helped.

Continue by briefly explaining how you became interested in his field, your education and most relevant strengths and skills, any work or volunteer experience you have already had in the field, and the steps you have taken to learn more, including the people in the field you have already met and the advice they have given you. Then ask five to eight carefully selected open-ended questions in priority order since you may never get to the last one if the other person's answers are long or he asks you lots of questions.

Select questions from the lists below to ask, noting the similarities and differences between the questions in the Discovery and Action steps. For example, in the Discovery step, you will want to ask questions about his field and industry, but in the Action step, you will want to ask questions about his specific company. If there are questions not listed here that you really need or want answered, be sure to include them. <u>Always make time to include a question at the end that asks the person you are meeting for additional people you should meet.</u>

Sample Questions to Ask During an Informational Interview

Discovery Step

- May I take a few minutes to tell you about my background? (He will say "of course.")

- Given what I have told you about myself, what jobs do you think I am best qualified for in your industry?

- What do you see as the main criteria for success in those jobs?

- How would you describe the industry culture?

- Do companies in your industry hire and/or sponsor international students on a short or long term basis?

- What's the best advice you can give me?

- Would you be willing to review and critique my resume?

- Would it be okay if I stay in touch with you to keep you updated on my job search?

- Who do you suggest I talk with next? May I use your name? (always try for at least two or three referrals)

Sample Questions to Ask During an Informational Interview

(Action Step)

- May I take a few minutes to tell you about my background? (He will say "of course.")

- Based upon what I have told you about myself, what jobs do you think I am best qualified for in your company?

- What qualifications does your company look for in a candidate for in the position we are discussing (skills, strengths, knowledge, education or certifications, experience)?

- How would you describe your company's culture?

- Would you be willing to review and critique my resume?

- Does your company hire international students on a short or long term basis? What else is important for me to know about the company?

- What's the best advice you can give me?

- Who do you suggest I talk with next? May I use your name? (always try for at least two or three referrals)

Q. Doesn't the person you are contacting for an informational interview assume that you want him to help you land a job?
A. Keep in mind that a job that is the wrong fit will not be sustainable, and that your main goal should be to ask questions that will allow you to determine your fit for the job, company, or industry. If the other person senses that you are sincerely interested in getting helpful career

information and advice, he will be less likely to question your motives. Your sincerity should come across when you ask for an informational interview and at the interview itself.

Q. Should I conduct myself differently than I would on a job interview?

A. No. The same basics apply. For example: be on time, make a compelling value statement, demonstrate strong interpersonal skills, and show him that you have researched his industry and company.

Q. What should I avoid saying?

A. Few people you plan to approach for job search help, including on an informational interview, will be interested in hearing about your personal wants or needs ("I am looking for a job as a marketing analyst, and I need to find a job before my student visa expires").

Your conversation should include your value statement, but do not take the time to give lots of details about your past job history, personal strengths, or accomplishments unless asked. Also, you should not ask him questions about current job openings unless he brings up the subject.

The Informational Interview Process

1. Send a LinkedIn Request to Connect (but don't ask for an informational interview)

Sample LinkedIn Request

Hi John, I was impressed by your profile on the Steinfeld Alumni page. I am a recent marketing graduate expanding my network with successful alumni in my field in New York City. I would be honored if you would accept this invitation to connect.

Thanks for considering!

Vivien

2. **Ask for the informational interview**

   <u>Once John accepts the LinkedIn invitation, you will have access to his email address under Contact Info on his Profile page.</u>
   Send an email or LinkedIn message with your reason for meeting and a suggested meeting place. You can use a standard format, but you should tailor your message for each situation.
   In your message:

   - Introduce yourself and mention how you originally got his name (e.g. referral, came across his LinkedIn profile while researching alumni or his industry, company or position). If possible, point out something you have in common.

   - Explain your reason for the request. <u>Only ask for information or advice</u>. If asking about a job is the focus of your call or email, and there are no posted openings, the person has a valid reason not to meet with you.

   - Suggest a 20 minute meeting at a coffee shop near his office since he will be less likely to be distracted, and more likely to engage in casual conversation, outside of his office. However, if he would rather meet at his office or somewhere away from his office, agree without objection.

Sample Email Requests:

Subj: Informational Interview Request

Hi John,

As I mentioned in my LinkedIn request, I came across your profile on the Steinfeld University alumni page on LinkedIn. I am a fellow alumnus who recently moved to NYC to pursue a career in marketing analytics or digital marketing.

It would be a great help if you would be kind enough to meet with me for 20 minutes over coffee near your office in the next week or two to answer a few questions about the lifestyle and job market in NYC, and offer me some advice. I have a temporary sales job, but will meet at your convenience if at all possible.

Thank you for considering my request.

Sincerely,

Vivien Zhu

Subj: Informational Interview Referral from Steven Steinfeld

Hi John,

A mutual friend, Steven Steinfeld, suggested that I contact you. I recently told him that I was interested in your industry and the kind of work that you do. I have researched your company and was impressed by what I read, especially when reading about the company's innovative new social media strategy.

As someone who is considering a career in your field, your insights would be extremely helpful as I plan my career path. For example, I would like to talk with you about some additional courses I'm thinking of taking to make me a more desirable candidate. To be clear, this is not a request for a job interview. I am truly interested in gaining some helpful information and advice.

I am available next Tuesday and Thursday. I promise to take no more than 20 minutes of your time.

Thank you for your consideration.

Sincerely,

Ping Huang

If you have a strong LinkedIn profile, he is likely to respond, but don't become frustrated if you do not get an immediate response. Some people will respond quickly, but many others will take time to respond, while others will need a reminder. If no response within ten days, forward your original email with the following heading and a similar message to the one in the example below:

Subj: Informational Interview Reminder

Dear John,

I'm not sure if you saw my request for a meeting for an informational interview, but I will be downtown next Tuesday and Thursday, and would be happy to buy you coffee between 2 and 4pm on either day if you are available. I promise to only take 20 minutes of your time to ask you a few questions and get some career advice. If you are too busy, I would appreciate it if you would recommend another successful person at your company with a similar background who might be available to meet with me.

Thanks again.

Vivian Zhu

Just send one reminder. Some people will never respond, but keep in mind that it's a numbers game. The more well written requests you send out, the greater the number of positive responses you will receive. Some people might say to follow up by phone, but I think it is better to follow up by email to eliminate any chance of miscommunication and to make it easier for the other person to respond.

3. **Prepare for the interview**

- Research the background of the person you will be interviewing on LinkedIn and through a Google search.
- Develop a set of questions as described earlier in this chapter.
- Remember that the person who you are talking with may be in a position to hire or recommend someone like you for a job in the near future. If so, they want to get to know you as much as they can in 20 or 30 minutes. Be prepared to give your value statement and success stories and answer questions such as why you are potentially interested in his company.
- Dress professionally, but in more casual dress than you would for a job interview (what we call "business casual").

4. **Hold the interview**

- Arrive at the meeting place 30 minutes early. Spend the time reviewing your research on the person you plan to interview and his company, and looking over your list of questions.
- You can have a mint to freshen your breath while you are waiting, but do not smoke before the interview or chew gum during the interview.
- When the other person arrives, greet him with a firm handshake while making eye contact, give him a BIG SMILE, and thank him for meeting with you.
- If you are in a coffee shop, ask him what he would like to eat or drink as soon as he arrives. Encourage him to order anything he wants. Order only coffee or tea for yourself, and be sure to pay for his as well as yours, even if he insists on paying.

- An informational interview should be thought of as a job interview, except that you are the one who starts the conversation by asking open-ended questions. Begin the conversation by reminding him of your purpose in getting together.

- Ask him friendly questions about his background before asking questions about industries, companies, or jobs.

- Bring your resume along, but don't take it out until he asks to see it. After looking over your resume, he may say something like, "Vivien, I'd like to show your resume to my boss (or send it to a friend). Do you happen to have a copy with you?" If this happens, thank him and ask him if he would be willing to make some resume recommendations before he sends it to anyone. If he has time, ask him to take a quick look on the spot. If not, send him your resume by email as soon as you get home. Either way, incorporate his best advice into your resume, and send him an updated resume attached to your thank you email.

- Listen for names of other people that he might mention who you might want to ask him to connect you to at the end of the conversation, "You mentioned Steven Steinfeld. Is he someone who might also give me helpful information or advice?"

- If the person you are interviewing likes you, and you are near his company's office, he may offer to have you accompany him to his office to show you around and maybe even meet a potential hiring manager before you leave. This is why you will want to suggest meeting near his office. It is also one of the reasons you will want to be well dressed. The other reason is that you don't know how he will be dressed, and you may feel uncomfortable if he is dressed professionally and you are dressed too casually.

- Remember that you only asked for 20 minutes. At the end of that time, thank the person and say that you have used up the promised amount of time, and start to get up to leave. If he is interested in what you have been saying, he may offer to give you some more time to ask a few more questions (a great sign).

5. **Follow-up After the Interview**

Send him a thank you email, such as the one in the following example, within 24-hours. Thank him again for his time and mention how much you enjoyed meeting him. Mention how much you appreciate the valuable information and referrals that he provided you, and that you will keep him posted as to your progress. Sign the note "Sincerely," and attach anything that he may have asked you to send him (e.g. resume, portfolio). If he is especially helpful, you may want to also send or deliver a hand-written note or small gift from your home country in addition to your email.

Dear Mr. Steinfeld,

Thank you very much for taking the time to meet with me on Thursday to discuss career possibilities in the media industry. I also appreciate your insights and advice, and was very impressed by your knowledge of the new and innovative ways social media is being utilized in the industry.

Thank you also for referring me to John Jones and Jim Smith. I have already contacted Mr. Smith at ABC Company, and we expect to meet next week. I plan to contact Mr. Jones tomorrow.

I will be in contact from time to time to keep you posted on my job search progress.

Thank you again for your help.

Sincerely.

Vivian Zhu

If you are not already connected on LinkedIn, send him a LinkedIn invitation to connect, and periodically send him an email about your job search or career progress, mentioning how you are putting his excellent advice and referrals to use. If possible, when following up, provide him with information that he might find helpful or interesting (e.g. by attaching a link to an article or event). <u>An informational interview may be a one-time event, but it can lead to a mutually beneficial long lasting relationship beyond your job search.</u> Also, keep in mind that if you meet with someone during your Discovery step, you may want to meet with him again when you are in your Action step.

If you see a job posting as this company that you think is a great fit for you, send the following email. If you have already identified a great job posting before the informational interview, don't mention it unless he asks since he may feel that this was your only reason for meeting.

Hi John,

Thanks again for the very helpful information and advice you offered at our meeting. Your company sounded so attractive that I checked the company website for postings that might be a great match for me and found the one in the following link (*insert link to posting*). I was going to send my resume to HR but I thought I might get much more attention and consideration if it came from you so I am attaching my resume and a cover letter. If this is asking too much, please let me know and I will apply online.

Thanks for considering!

Vivian

Wondering why professionals in your field would be willing to meet you? Here are ten reasons you will be granted an informational (or job) interview:

1. As a favor for a friend, relative, or another employee.

2. The employee stands to get a referral bonus if he recommends you and you are hired.

3. Your compelling value statement.

4. You mention information or ideas that may be helpful to the hiring manager or the organization.

5. You have a common background or interests. These can be culture, work or school related. If he was an international student himself, he may want to give back for the help he received when he was looking for a job.

6. He knows about an unannounced staffing need that you might fit. This is what you are hoping for since the company would rather not go through an expensive and lengthy job search process if it can be avoided.

7. He was flattered when you mentioned that you want to talk to him because he is a highly respected person in his industry or company.

8. He loves to give advice and guidance (many professionals do). Using the expression, "I need your help," often leads to a positive result.

9. He is instructed to meet with you by his boss. For example, a very good approach if you do not have a contact in common is to contact a senior executive. If you want to get to the Materials Engineering Manager who works for the General Manager, contact the General Manager. There is a good chance that you will be redirected to a lower level of management ("Thank you for your interest in our company. I suggest that you contact the Materials Engineering Manager"). Now, when you email the Materials Engineering

Manager, you can honestly say that the General Manager suggested you contact him. Even if he does not instruct someone to interview you, there is a good chance that he will refer your resume to the HR department where it may get special attention.

10. He has an interest in your culture. He may even be planning to visit your country in the near future.

Common Informational Interview Mistakes

* Lack of preparation.

* Arriving late for the interview. Unlike in some other countries, punctuality in U.S. business is expected and highly valued.

* Acting too quiet, formal or overly respectful.

* Wasting time by not staying on topic. You only have 20 minutes, and it goes by quickly. Use it wisely!

* Mentioning your weaknesses.

* Asking unnecessary, closed-ended, or time consuming questions

* Taking more than the requested amount of time without permission.

* Asking for a job.

- Forgetting to ask for additional informational interview referrals.

- No thank you note (or a poorly written one).

- Not following up or staying in touch.

Accept all informational interviews offered, even when you think that they will not provide valuable information or lead to a job offer you might accept. You may be surprised by the results. If nothing else, they will give you a great way to practice your interviewing skills.

Mastering Job Interviews

"You never get a second chance to make a first impression."

– Will Rogers, U.S. Humorist

The goal of an in-person interview is to gain insight into your personality, strengths, work behaviors and values, since the interviewer already has a good idea about your skills, knowledge and experience from your resume (and possibly a telephone or Skype interview).

Basic hiring criteria can be expressed in terms of seven words beginning with the letter "C". You should also be looking at these same seven criteria to personally assess your fit for the position.

1. Are you **Competent** to hold the job?

   Do you meet the hiring criteria for this job? If they have brought you in for an interview, they certainly feel that you can probably meet the job requirements, and are hoping that you can exceed the requirements without being overqualified.

2. Are you **Compatible** with the culture of the organization?

    If you are being considered for employment, your culture is probably valued by the company. It may be more important for you to assess how comfortable you will feel within the company's culture. It's helpful to look around to get a sense of the diversity, ages and styles of dress of the people you pass on the way in and out of the office.

3. Will it be easy to **Communicate** with you and you with us?

    Do you have enough of a grasp of English to be able to communicate easily and effectively with your supervisor, colleagues, and teammates when necessary? Speak very slowly and clearly since it takes time for Americans to adjust to what we call a "foreign accent." Speak especially slowly when making an important point about your background, skills, strengths, and accomplishments.

    Do not confuse interpersonal skills (ability to get along well with others) with communication skills (the ability to absorb and communicate ideas so that other people easily grasp your meaning). Sometimes international students tell an interviewer that they have good communication skills when they mean interpersonal skills. If your communication skills are not strong, you can still do well on the interview if you make the case for employment by virtue of your other skills and strengths. If you have passed a telephone interview and/or the job does not require a lot of verbal communication, you should not worry about your English language skills.

    Your ability to hold your own in a two-way conversation with the interviewer will be another indicator of your communication skills.

112

4. Do you have **Chemistry** with the hiring manager?

Do you have chemistry with your prospective new boss during the interview? If not, ask why not? If you will be working closely with him, and feel that you will have a hard time forming a working relationship, you may want to seek a different opportunity. Generally speaking, the hiring manager will connect with people in his own image, so you will want to do your best mirror his communication style. For example, if he has an outgoing, strong personality, you may want to talk more, and with more authority, than you would normally.

It is very important to be likeable. A hiring manager will not hire a candidate that he doesn't like, but will hire a candidate he likes very much even if that candidate is lacking in other ways. Show your personality! If he likes you, he will be looking for reasons to hire you. If he doesn't, he will be looking for reasons NOT to hire you. **Make him fall in love with you. If he does, you are almost certain to get a job offer.**

5. Do you have **Confidence** that you can do the job with excellence?

No one will hire you if you do not exhibit 100% confidence in your ability to get the job done. If you can only bring one thing with you to a job interview, make it confidence. When talking about yourself, use words like "excellent," "outstanding," and "exceptional." If you have a hard time using those words when describing your strengths and skills, say that other people use those words when describing your skills. In a competitive job market, employers don't hire "good" interns or employees; they hire potentially "great" ones.

6. Will you make a measurable **Contribution**?

Beyond just meeting the basic job responsibilities, will you help the employer meet the goals and challenges of the organization?

Put yourself in the shoes of the hiring manager. He wants to hire achievers who go far beyond their basic job duties to help the company (and his department) achieve its goals (e.g. revenue growth, profitability, cost savings, client and employee satisfaction). Impress the interviewer by delivering prepared C.A.R. stories.

C.A.R. stands for Challenge, Action, and Result. Prepare C.A.R. stories that talk about your greatest accomplishments and major strengths, and find a time to comfortably fit them into the conversation. For example, if you are a problem solver, give a C.A.R. story that gives an example of a time you used that strength. If you have researched the company, include C.A.R. stories that talk about how you helped former employers overcome challenges similar to the ones that the company (or department) is currently facing.

In any case, talk less about challenges and results, and more about your actions. Practice your C.A.R. stories so that you can tell them in less than two minutes. If it is too long, the hiring manager may have a hard time following your story.

The following is an example of a C.A.R. story:

(**Challenge**) "Because they were using an outdated survey form, my department was in danger of missing their client satisfaction goals for the year.

(**Action**) I developed a new, more comprehensive, customer satisfaction survey and contacted our top 50 customers to ask them to quickly complete and return it.

(**Result**) When we included these surveys in our final results, we had achieved a record high score of 4.5 on a scale of one to five."

7. Are your **Compensation** expectations in line with the budget?

    Just as you should not bring up the visa issue, you should also
    not bring up compensation during an interview. If the interviewer
    brings it up, just say that you are "flexible" or "open," or "more
    concerned about finding the right fit." For more on this subject, see
    the chapter titled *Negotiating Your Salary*.

Beyond the 7 C's

At the entry level, it is very important to stress your **strong work ethic**
(and that you intend to go above and beyond what is expected), ability to
work well with others, and **self-motivation and drive**. When applying
for an internship, stress that you need little supervision since interns have
the potential to take up a great deal of supervisory time with a relatively
low return to the company.

You will want to pay special attention to the characteristics listed
below. <u>Even though some employers will value some of these attributes as
more important than others, none are unimportant, and exhibiting the top
three listed (passion, enthusiasm, and positive attitude) will always help
your interview.</u> Of course, if you can find out which are most important to
the hiring manager through an informational interview, you can focus more
attention on those.

Passion

Employers will respond very positively if you mention that you are
passionate about your career, mainly because they expect that passionate
people will work very hard.

Enthusiasm

In addition to showing enthusiasm for the position, show enthusiasm for the organization's products or services, mission, vision and goals. As with passion, this will send the message that you plan to work hard. If you need to fake enthusiasm, you may want to look for another opportunity.

Positive Attitude

If an employer had to choose between a candidate with an outstanding school or work record but a less than positive attitude and a lesser candidate with an exceptionally positive attitude, he would choose the one with the better attitude.

Global Thinking

This refers not only to your ability to bring an international perspective to the company (**an advantage over many American students**), but also to your ability to think across boundaries (department, company, industry, geography) in bringing valuable new ideas to your job or the company. Present yourself as someone constantly seeking better ways to improve results and the work environment.

Integrity and Honesty

These qualities draw people to you and make you an effective team member or team leader.

Determination and Commitment

Get across that you will find a way to achieve and exceed every goal and meet every challenge, overcoming all obstacles put in your way, and you will have an excellent chance of being selected.

Adaptability/Flexibility/Resilience

This refers to your ability to respond quickly and positively to changes in the environment, and your help in creating necessary change.

Time Management

Express that you do not like to waste time, are always looking for ways to save time (after all, time is money), and that you are also looking for ways to help your fellow employees save time.

Accountability

Show that you take responsibility for your results, including your past failures. You will also want to show that you learned from your mistakes and failures.

Quality

Express that you value quality and want to excel in an organization that values quality (which is one reason you chose to apply to this organization).

Team Playing

A true team player actively pursues the goals of the team regardless of the impact on his own personal interests.

Leadership

Everyone is expected to step up as needed to provide team leadership. Leaders do not have to have a management title. Any employee can lead by setting a positive example, and by driving others to achieve the organization's mission and goals.

Learning

It's particularly important for all young professionals, and especially technology professionals, to get across that they are eager to learn, and that can absorb, apply, and communicate new knowledge quickly and effectively with limited or no formal training.

Problem Solving

A critical thinker considers facts that are not obvious, actively seeks solutions from others, solves problems creatively, and identifies potential problems. **Although not expected in entry level employees in some cultures, critical thinking skills are expected and highly valued by employers in the U.S.**

Mentorship

If you are good with technology, mention that you have the capability and willingness to mentor your co-workers who may be having difficulty in adapting to new technologies.

Before the Day of the Interview

Research the Company

You can do this through a Google Advanced Search, on LinkedIn, by reading the latest annual report, looking at recent news and analysis on the industry and company (www.reportlinker.com), and through informational interviews.

Research Your Interviewers

Find out as much as you can about your potential interviewers' reputations, personalities, management styles, hobbies, accomplishments, immediate needs, expertise, work histories, and hot button issues. Use Google Advanced Search, LinkedIn, and informational interviews. Make sure that you have the correct spelling of your interviewers' names and current titles.

Take Note of Time and Location

If possible, schedule a time when you are typically at your best (e.g. morning). In any event, schedule the interview on a day or time that will comfortably allow you to arrive near the interview location one hour before the interview.

Double check that you have the correct address of the location where you will be meeting since the company may have multiple offices in the same geography or may have moved recently. Make sure you know how to get there and give yourself extra time in case of transportation or other unexpected delay.

Confirm the Interview

If you have more than one day's notice, send an e-mail to the person who scheduled the interview the day before the interview confirming the day, place, and time. This will not only make you look professional, but may help you avoid an embarrassing or costly mistake if you have written down the wrong day, place, or time.

Subj: Interview Confirmation

Dear Ms. Jones,

I am confirming my interview with Mr. Steinfeld for tomorrow, June 4th at 3pm at your office on the 19th floor of 1440 Illinois Place. If the time or date needs to be rescheduled, please contact me at 888-888-8888. I look forward to meeting you when I arrive for the interview.

Thank you.

Vivian Zhu

Prepare Your Resume and Portfolio

Prepare five extra copies of your most recently updated resume to take with you, and offer one to everyone who interviews you, "I have a clean copy of my updated resume with me. Would you like a copy?" If you have a portfolio with examples of exemplary work (that's not violating the confidentiality of your former employers), bring it along and find a good time to show it, "Mr. Steinfeld, Rather than tell you about the ad campaign that I helped put together for ABC Industries, I brought along a copy to show you."

If you are showing your portfolio to demonstrate your creativity, remember to explain how your creativity helped to achieve business goals.

Practice Your Answers

If your school offers mock interviews, take advantage of that opportunity. If not, practice your answers to common interview questions with a friend who will give you honest feedback. Common interview questions, in addition to the ones in this book, can easily be found on the Internet. Be sure to especially practice your answer to the first commonly asked question, "Please tell me about yourself," and your C.A.R. stories until they seem unrehearsed. Your answers should be easy to understand, related to the question, and focused on your accomplishments. Don't memorize your answers, but reduce each one to a few bullet points that you can keep in your head at interviews.

Prepare Your Questions

Prepare the questions that you will ask the interviewer during the course of the interview, paying special attention to the questions that you are expected to ask at the end of the interview. I offer you some good possibilities later in this chapter. Keep in mind that if you have no or few questions, he may think that you are not particularly interested in the job or company. Do not ask the interviewer if his company sponsors international students since this may make him think that you are more interested in getting a visa than contributing to the company.

Prepare Your Wardrobe

Always have your interview clothing ready to go in case you are called for an interview on short notice. Even if the company has a casual dress policy, dress conservatively in quality clothing for the interview, but set yourself apart from the ultra-conservative black suit and white shirt or blouse that many international students wear. If you are a man, wear an all-season black, grey or dark blue suit, but spruce it up with a light blue or stripped shirt and a simple but colorful patterned tie. If you are a woman, I suggest that you wear a dark skirt or suit, but spruce it up with a colorful blouse. Wear stylish but conservative leather shoes that match your suit (with black socks if you are a man). It is also very important that your suit or skirt and shirt or blouse fit you very well. I suggest that you have your suits professionally tailored when you buy them, your interview clothes professionally cleaned and pressed, and your interview shoes kept highly polished and in excellent condition. The most important thing about how you look for an interview is to feel confident when you walk out your door. If you don't, you may need to reevaluate how you are dressed or groomed.

The Day of the Interview

Stay high energy, but control nervousness. It will help your composure and confidence if you arrive at a local coffee shop near the interview site an hour or more before the interview is scheduled to begin.

When you are settled in at the coffee shop, write down the 3 Unique Selling Points (USPs) you want to make sure you get across at the interview (e.g. passionate about marketing analytics, 3 successful internships, and Case competition awards). Follow this activity by reviewing your research on the company and interviewers, and by taking a final look at the job description. Before leaving the coffee shop, write down a few of your C.A.R. stories in bullet form to anchor positive thoughts. Arrive at the company 15 minutes early for the interview, immediately take off your outerwear and make a quick trip to the rest room to check your appearance.

Put on a smile when you enter the office, be especially nice to everyone on the way in and out of the office, and engage the receptionist while you are in the reception area. You never know who might comment about you to the interviewer after you leave. "Was Vivian Zhu here for an interview? I really liked her." If the interviewer is unsure about hiring you or someone else, a positive comment from another person might tip the balance in your favor.

Turn off your cell phone, and when called to enter the office to meet the interviewer, do so without hesitation. Greet the interviewer with a friendly smile (that you should keep going throughout the interview), a firm handshake, energy, a confident posture with your shoulders back, and direct eye contact. Put down your briefcase or folder, and sit down at a comfortable distance with your back straight and your knees facing the interviewer.

Ace the Interview

Pay Close Attention to Your Surface Indicators

These include your appearance, personality, attentive listening, and verbal communication skills. Your tone of voice, facial movements and body language can be more important than the actual words you say. This is another reason to pursue only jobs that are an excellent fit. **If you want to "sound" genuinely confident and enthusiastic, you need to "be" genuinely confident and enthusiastic.**

Be Genuine

Be yourself, not what you may think the interviewer wants you to be. Any sign of insincerity will create doubt in the mind of the hiring manager about everything you say.

Control Your Nerves

A certain amount of nervous energy can give you a performance edge, but don't allow nervousness to make you fidget or turn you into a robot.

Align Your Value

The way to score a winning interview is to align your value with the organization's immediate needs, goals and challenges. This is one of the most important things that you can do on an interview, and why you need to spend whatever time is necessary to research the company completely.

Take Control of the Interview

No matter which question is asked, answer the question but direct your answers as much as possible to the 3 unique selling points (USPs) you want to get across to your interviewer that will make you stand out from other candidates and make you memorable. Think of a politician. When interviewed, a politician will often add a few points to his answer that he wants to make sure he gets across even if they are not directly related to the original question.

Be Conversational

Go out of your way to be conversational and show your personality. If you are super friendly or humorous by nature, show it! It will make you more likeable and more memorable.

Keep Your Answers Short and Direct

When possible, keep your answers under one minute and ALWAYS under two minutes. If you talk any longer, the interviewer may lose interest in what you are saying, you may sound inarticulate, or you may wind up sounding less than confident in your answer. **Do not worry about being too assertive or self-promoting. In the U.S., direct answers are expected, and will not present a problem as long as you remain polite and respectful in your responses.**

Always Respond with Positive and Confident Answers

Be positive at all times. This is not the time to be humble or compare your abilities to someone with more experience. **You must make the case that you are an exceptionally strong candidate every minute of the interview.** Do not say something like, "I am very knowledgeable about marketing but wish I knew more about forecasting." Simply say, "I am very knowledgeable about marketing," and stop talking. If you are asked about something that did not work out well, take the opportunity to discuss a turn-around situation in which a poor start ended in a positive outcome.

Actively Listen

Show interest in the interviewer and what he has to say by actively listening much more than you talk. Rephrase and summarize as necessary to understand and clarify questions. Maintain eye contact and be patient.

Watch for Non-Verbal Cues

Is the interviewer leaning forward? If yes, he is interested in what you are saying. Or, is he leaning back with eyes glazing over? Is he sitting in an open, receptive position or sitting with his shoulder turned toward you or with his arms folded and feet crossed? If you are getting negative cues, you may want to shorten your answers and start asking questions to engage the interviewer.

Summarize the Meeting

Start with expressing your interest and enthusiasm for both the company and position, followed by how you can contribute to meeting the goals or challenges of the organization, "Thank you for meeting with me today. I'm not only excited about the job, but impressed by what you've told me about the organization. I hope you agree that my skills, knowledge, and attention to detail can help contribute to your development of an improved accounting system."

Speak to Your Resume

They were impressed enough with your resume to ask you to interview. The interviewer's questions will let you know what stood out. Be very familiar with every line in your resume, and anticipate questions, including questions about your extracurricular activities.

Non-Traditional In-Person Interviews

When we think of interviewing, we naturally think of a traditional one-on-one interview with the hiring manager or a series of in-person interviews leading up to the final decision maker; but there are a growing number of different types of interviews that you may be exposed to during your career. The key is to basically handle them in the same way as you would a traditional interview, but with an awareness of the differences explained below.

Panel Interviews

Don't get nervous if there is more than one interviewer in the room. This could signal insecurity in any one individual's interviewing ability, the need to save time in the interviewing process, or wanting to come to a quick consensus, "I liked Vivian. What did you guys think of her? Do we agree that she is one of our top candidates?" Focus on making sure that you address each person in the group, keep your answers short and to the point so as not to lose anyone's interest, and spend more time making eye contact with the key decision makers. Some group interviews are meant to be "stress interviews" where your composure and confidence are under examination, so be sure to keep your cool.

Group Interviews

If you arrive to find yourself one of multiple candidates to be interviewed at the same time, don't be intimidated. Just remember to speak up when it is your turn, and listen carefully to what everyone else is saying since it will help you to form your answers and avoid repeating what others have said. Above all, stay confident and remember to focus your answers on your Unique Selling Points.

Informal Interviews

If you get invited to a lunch or coffee, order the same thing that the interviewer orders (or something at similar cost), avoid alcoholic beverages, and stay very mindful of your table manners. If you are unsure of U.S. table manners, research them online before your meeting (http://www.tripadvisor.com/Travel-g191-c58158/United-States:Polite.Manners.html).

Don't lower your guard because of the informal atmosphere. Give the same answers that you would give in a more formal environment.

Telephone and Skype Interviews

Prior to an in-person interview, you may be asked to participate in a telephone interview. This type of interview is typically led by an HR professional in a large company, and a hiring manager in a small company. The purpose is to reduce the number of candidates invited to meet with the management team in person.

Although you may get a few behavioral questions in a telephone interview, you can expect it to be mainly focused on the facts contained in your resume. Since the interview will only be scheduled for 20 or 30 minutes, you will need to be well prepared to answer questions with little hesitation. Give this interview the same weight as an in-person interview. Keep in mind that you will not be taking the next step if you are not one of the top candidates after all their telephone interviews are completed.

They have asked you to the telephone interview because they suspect that you have the background needed to be successful—but you will be expected to build a strong case for being hired—and defend and expand on every accomplishment bullet in your resume.

Preparing for a Telephone Interview

Keep the following within easy reach:

- Your resume
- Company research
- Your C.A.R. stories (in bullet form)
- The job posting. Mark it up in green, yellow, and red as discussed in the chapter titled The 3 Steps. Pay special attention to where you are strongest and weakest. Bring the conversation back to your strongest qualifications as often as possible and do not mention your weaknesses.
- Your 3 Unique Selling Points. The same interviewers may be conducting several telephone interviews in a row, and you want them to remember you when they get together to discuss who will be selected for an in-person interview ("Vivian Zhu? I remember her well. She was the one who is passionate about marketing analytics, had internships in the U.S. and the UK, and won awards in Case competitions.")
- Written answers (in bullet form) to questions about your resume, skills, strengths, and background that you might expect to receive.
- Questions to ask the interviewer (see examples later in this chapter).

Telephone Interview Tips

These tips are in addition to the basic interview tips shared later in this chapter

- When first contacted, ask for an in-person interview if the interviewer is in your same city. They may turn you down, but it is worth a try.
- If you are called without warning, even if you are available, explain that it is an inconvenient time, and schedule a time later in the day or the next day when you will be better prepared.

- Be aware of possible time differences. If the caller is in New York City, but you are in Chicago, the time of the interview will be different in each city.
- Take the call from a private, quiet location with excellent cell phone reception.
- Smile as much as possible throughout the call.
- Be careful not to interrupt.
- Speak clearly, confidently, and VERY SLOWLY—and don't allow your voice to trail off at the end of a sentence. No matter how slowly you think you are talking, you will be talking more quickly than you think. Speak especially slowly when mentioning something important that you want to get across.
- Do your best to put your complete and focused attention on what the interviewer is saying rather than focusing on your prepared materials.

Phone Interview Questions

The following are examples of questions you may get on a phone interview. Although you may be asked some of the same behavioral questions asked at an in-person interview, there will be more questions focused on your resume, your understanding of the job, and your ability to do the job with excellence. You will also probably get some of the same questions on a Skype interview that you will get on a telephone interview.

- Tell me about your education, skills, strengths and experience as it relates to this job.
- Tell me what you did at your internship at (ABC) company?
- Tell me about a time that you participated in a team. What did you contribute?

- Why do you think you will be successful at this job?
- What do you know about our company?
- What type of work environment do you prefer?
- What requirements of this job are you unsure or less confident about?

Skype Interviews

Many companies are moving from phone to Skype interviews in order to simulate more of an in-person interview experience. Prepare for a Skype interview in much the same way that you would an in-person interview.

Skype Interview Tips

These tips are in addition to the telephone interview tips above and basic interview tips later in this chapter

- Split your screen to have access to a few very important notes that you many want to refer to during the call without looking down, but only glance at them if absolutely necessary since you will want to keep steady eye contact into the camera as much as possible.
- Dress business casual in muted colors, and pay special attention to your grooming.
- When preparing for the interview, choose your location carefully. Set up a Skype call in advance with a friend to practice and help set your camera's positioning in the room. Use a private room with good lighting, and make sure that the interviewer is not going to be distracted by anything in the background, including pets.
- If you might be disturbed, put a "Do Not Disturb – Interview in Progress" sign on the door.

- Sit at a desk or table.

- Check your Internet connection.

- Turn off any other programs running on your computer – you don't want to be distracted by an email suddenly popping up while you are speaking.

- Speak CLEARLY and SLOWLY into the microphone.

- Make sure that you have a phone number and/or email for your interviewer, so that you can contact him if you run into any technical issues.

- At the end of the interview, wait for the other party to log off, and double check that you are logged off before you get up from your chair.

- Whether inside or outside the U.S., always suggest a Skype rather than a phone interview since it will give you the chance to make more of a personal connection with the interviewer.

In-Person Interview Q's and A's

You should always be prepared to answer questions that are very specific to the job, particularly if you are interviewing with the hiring manager. However, you also need to prepare for common open-ended questions that are important to all interviewers. Below, are some of these questions that I have found to be particularly challenging for international students. Some of these are behavioral questions meant to uncover how you acted in specific situations in the past. The logic is that past performance is likely to repeat in the future. I have included the interviewer's probable thinking behind the questions (shown in parentheses).

You may pick up ideas for answers from these examples or the hundreds of others you can find on the Internet, but avoid copying some else's exact

<u>responses</u>. Be sure that your answers are aligned with your own personality and situation.

The first ten questions below are the ones that I use with international students in mock interviews because they are often asked in one form or another at in-person job interviews, and sometimes in phone or Skype interviews. By the time I hear the answers to the first five questions, I am fairly clear on the candidate's chances for the job. **By the time we finish all ten questions, and I hear the interviewee's questions for me** (explained a little later in this chapter)—**I feel that I can predict his chances of being offered the job with 100% certainty.**

Q1. Please tell me about yourself (Please tell me why are you qualified for this job. Focus on only the highlights in your resume and information that I can't get from your resume that I may find interesting).
A. This is often the first question asked and your answer can set the tone for the entire interview. The interviewer is not looking for a rehash of the basic information in your resume (which he may be looking at as he speaks with you). He is looking for a summary of the reasons he should consider hiring you—and is also testing your verbal communication skills. You can answer this important question by following the sample format below:

"**I'm a** (recent business school graduate) **with a passion for** (data analysis and marketing). **I chose to study** (marketing) **because** I have always had an interest in (data and consumer **behavior**). **I am strong at** (SPSS and Advanced Excel), **and have often been told that I have excellent** (teamwork, and problem solving skills). **I demonstrated these skills in** (three very successful internships and several school projects). **I also** (studied piano for many years). **I bring the same** (discipline) **to everything I do.**"

Q2. Why did you choose to major in (accounting)? (Are you enthusiastic about your field of study or have you been pushed into it by a parent or someone else?).

A. Don't just say, "My father is an accountant and encouraged me to follow a similar career." Your answer should be interesting and show that you are following your strengths and interests, such as "I have loved playing with numbers since I was a little boy, and was always an outstanding student in math. My passion for numbers led me to major in accounting. Even when I am not in school or working, I like to do problem solving numbers puzzles like Sudoku." In any event, you should include the answer to this question as part of your response to "Tell me about yourself." If you mention a parent's business, be sure to say that while your parent's business may have encouraged you to enter the field, you are not planning to return home to join their business.

Q3. Why are you interested in working for this company? (Are you applying to a million companies or are you being selective? Also, convince me that you've researched us.)

A. Do not make meaningless statements such as "I love to travel." Instead say something like, "I've been interested in the financial services industry since my internship at Steinfeld Bank. I've researched this company both online and through informational interviews with some of your current and past employees. I believe that your goals and team-oriented culture fit well with the type of job and organization where I can fit in well and make an immediate contribution. For example, I found out that you are expanding your social networking presence. Social networking is one of my passions."

Q4. What are your greatest strengths? (Do you have the soft skills necessary to be successful at this particular job?)

A. "I have been told that my top strengths are my analytical, problem solving, and leadership skills. My manager at my last internship also mentioned my passion for marketing as one of my greatest strengths."

Q5. What would you say is your number one weakness? (Everyone has weaknesses. Apart from not speaking perfect English, tell me about one that can negatively affect the quality of your work or your productivity. Tell me how you are working to make it less of a problem).

A. Do not talk about a weaknesses or lack of experience, and do not repeat the word "weakness." <u>If you actually talk about a real weakness, it may be all the interviewer remembers at the end of the interview.</u> Instead, give a short answer about how you sometimes overuse one of your strengths and mention that you have worked to overcome that challenge, "One of my greatest strengths is my attention to detail. However, sometimes I spend an unnecessary amount of time checking for errors. This is something I have been working hard to change. Instead of checking my work three or four times, I now only check it once or twice."

Q6. Please tell me about one of your favorite projects at work or school? (What type of work do you really enjoy? The more you enjoy the work, the more you will be engaged in the work and the better job you will do).

A. This can be one of the most important questions you will be asked since it will provide the interviewer with exceptional insight into your skills and strengths. When answering this questions, don't forget to explain "Why" this was your favorite project. It's best to use a work example, but you can also use a school project, "I was assigned to a team in a competition to create financial models. Although I am one of the best students in my class in VBA, I was not as expert in MATLAB. I studied MATLAB all night so that I could make a significant contribution to the team immediately. In the end, our team won first prize. This was my favorite project because it allowed me to test my ability to learn quickly, and also because it helped me become very good in the MATLAB programming language."

Q7. Please tell me about a difficult challenge you faced at work or school, and how you handled it (Give me a C.A.R. story about your greatest accomplishment at an internship, job or volunteer activity. If you have no work accomplishments, talk about a time you overcame a challenge at school or at a volunteer or extracurricular activity. Keep in mind that I am also interested in understanding what you consider to be a "difficult" challenge).

A. "I was hired as a marketing intern, and was given the challenge to analyse the company's top competitor's social media strategy. I took the initiative to execute an in-depth analysis of the company's top five competitors, and was very proud when they decided to use my results as the basis for a new revenue generating social media campaign. In addition to making a contribution to the company, I learned a lot about the retail industry from that experience."

Q8. Tell me about a failure or mistake you made during an internship or job (Do you learn from your mistakes and can you quickly recover from them? Do you take responsibility for failure or blame someone or something else?).

A. "When I was an intern, my department failed in meeting a project goal on time. I learned something about time management from that experience; and even though I was only an intern, I took my share of the responsibility along with the rest of the team."

Q9. What do you think you will be doing five years from now? (Do you have realistic expectations? Might you want to work with our company? Are you planning to return to your home country?)

A. Do not talk about going back to your home country after a few years even if that is your intention right now. If you think it will help you to say that you plan to go back to school for an advanced degree, say that you intend to get this degree in evening classes after work and study on weekends. You are not hiding the truth. The future is hard to predict and your plans may change. Give the interviewer the impression that there is a chance that you would like to be with his company in five years, even if you are interviewing for an internship, "It's difficult to look that far ahead, but this appears to be a great company. If I am working here in five years,

I don't know what my job title would be, but I expect that I would be taking on much more responsibility by that time."

Q10. Why should we hire you rather than one of our other excellent candidates? What's special about you? (I don't want to make a mistake, so help me justify hiring you to my senior management. Tell me in not too many words why you are exceptionally suited for this internship or job?)
A. This is often the last question asked, and may represent your last chance to summarize your case for being hired. "Based upon what I know about the job, I believe that I have an excellent mix of strengths, skills, and knowledge to do an outstanding job. I don't know how good your other candidates are with Microsoft Excel and Access, but I am outstanding at both. I also believe that my enthusiasm for the company and the position will show up in my commitment to doing the best job possible. As a start, I believe that I can make an immediate contribution to setting up the new reporting structure that you mentioned."

Q11. Are you authorized to work and accept new employment in the United States?
A. An interviewer is not supposed to ask you about your national origin, current immigration status, specific documents, or the duration or legal basis for any current work authorization you may have; and will typically not ask to see proof of work authorization until after they make you a job offer. However, the interviewer can legally ask you if you are authorized to work in the U.S., and some interviewers who are unfamiliar with the law may ask you questions they should not be asking. Do not bring visa questions up, but be prepared to respond without hesitation when asked. If you are a student or recent graduate only interested in working under OPT, just say "Yes" if asked if you are authorized to work in the U.S. If you are asked if you will need sponsorship at some point, you should be ready to explain the process in broad terms, and say something like "I will need

an H-1B visa to extend my stay in the U.S. for three years and beyond. As you may know, the process requires that the company file a petition on my behalf. My goal is to work hard and earn consideration for sponsorship since I would like to stay with the company long term." (See the chapter titled *Visa Laws and Your Work Options*)

Interview Questions Testing Critical Thinking Ability

Usually critical thinking is tested only during technical interviews, but sometimes the interviewer may test your critical thinking during a non-technical interview. There is almost no limit to the number of questions that can be asked to test your problem solving ability. A couple of real life interview examples are, "How would you cure world hunger?" and "How many people are using Facebook on a Friday at 2:30pm in San Francisco?" and "If you were an ingredient in a Big Mac, which ingredient would you be?"

Here are three rules of thumb to keep in mind when answering, since the answer is less important than the thought process:

1. You've been given everything you need to give an answer
2. Speak your thoughts out loud so that the interviewer can hear the process you are using to try to find the answer
3. Sometimes the best answer might be to say that you would do a Google search

Questions to Ask the Interviewer

Finding meaningful questions to ask at the end of the interview is usually the most difficult part of the interview for international students. You can overcome this, and stand out from other candidates, if you prepare questions to ask in advance.

You don't need to wait to the end of the interview to ask questions, but the interviewer will always ask you if you have any questions before ending the interview ("Do you have any questions for me?"). Interviewers will actually appreciate questions at any point in the interview if they are not very experienced at interviewing and are struggling to find questions to ask you.

Don't ask more than four questions in a row, and **don't ask questions that make it appear that you are more concerned with what you want from the job** (e.g. experience, knowledge, a high salary, or training) **than making a contribution to the goals of the organization.**

Don't ask questions such as "What will I be doing in a typical day?" or "What is my work schedule?" or "What do you expect of me?" **Your questions should demonstrate that you are focused on adding value rather than on routine activities.** Also, do not ask questions about the organization that you could have gotten easily from the company website or that ask about the company's high level strategy. **Keep to questions that show that you are focused on the job and needs of the department under discussion.**

The following are types of other questions that I often hear at mock interviews that are NOT particularly helpful to leaving the best impression:

- How do you like working for the company? (Leave this type of question for informational interviews).
- How do I fit into the organization? (You should be telling the interviewer, not asking)
- Please rate me with other candidates on a scale of 1-10 (You can ask how you compare to other candidates he has seen, but do not put him on the spot by asking for a number. In any event, he will not give you one).

Below are ten good questions that you might consider using at an in-person job interview. Select three to six (including #2, #4 and #9) to ask:

1. What are the 3 top criteria you are looking for in a candidate? If possible, ask this early in the interview. If you can start the conversation by asking the interviewer to explain the most important success factors in the job under discussion, you will have a huge advantage since you will be able to align your answers with his criteria. If he responds that this was laid out in the job description, tell him that you are familiar with the job description but that you would like his personal viewpoint.

2. Can you please describe the culture of the organization? What types of people are happiest and most successful working here?

3. What are the department's immediate goals and challenges?

4. I'm an achiever. What would be important for me to accomplish in my first month? What about long term (or by the end of my internship)?

5. What do I need to do to be the best intern (employee) that you have ever had?

6. From everything that I went over, does it seem like I'm the type of employee (or intern) you are looking for? This will allow you one last chance to clear up any misunderstandings and restate your case for employment if necessary. His answer might also help you do better in your next interview.

7. Ask at least one question that shows that you have researched the company (e.g. I have been researching your company online, and have a question about your social media strategy.)

8. Is there anything about my skills or my background that you would like me to clarify?

9. I am very excited about the organization and the job. What are the next steps in the interview process?

10. What is the best way to follow up with you?

Basic Interview Tips

- If you have an American name or nickname, use it.
- Use Mr or Ms when addressing the interviewer, rather than Sir or Madam. If the interviewer is young and friendly, ask if you can call him by his first name.
- Keep your hands away from your face and your mouth, and avoid excessive gesturing.
- Do not remain overly soft spoken or quiet out of respect for the interviewer. It may come across as a lack of confidence.
- Don't use the word "We" too often. American companies are interested in what you did more than what the team accomplished. Use the word "I" as much as possible.
- Avoid apologizing or being defensive about things you can't change (your age, education, level of experience, visa status).

- Don't take notes, except to write down important names and positions that may come up during the interview on a small pad.
- Turn off your phone and put it away before the interview.
- Don't look at your watch during the interview, even if you are curious as to the time. You may appear to be bored.
- Be sure to collect the business cards of everyone you meet.
- Make every word count. Avoid using filler words such as "like," "umm," or "you know."
- Speak slowly and pause to give the interviewer time to reflect on what you are saying, particularly when you are saying something important.
- If your interviewer is speaking very quickly, do NOT speed up. Instead, shorten your answers to help increase the pace of conversation.
- Avoid discussing politics or other subjects that might be controversial. If the interviewer brings uncomfortable subjects up during small talk at the beginning of the interview, change the subject.
- If the interviewer asks you a sensitive question that you think is inappropriate (e.g. religion, marital status, physical disabilities), respond with "Is this relevant to the position?" He will likely withdraw the question.
- Do not mention diversity as a reason to hire you. You will probably not qualify as a diversity candidate, and it is not a reason that they will hire you.
- Since recruitment and training are expensive, don't mention going back to your home country or back to school full-time.

- Limit non-relevant school talk. Only talk about classes where you excelled and are relevant to the job.

- Stress your drive and ambition but be careful not to give the impression that you plan to use this job as a launching pad for bigger and better things in the very near future.

- Listen carefully to the questions so that you do not give a non-relevant answer. For instance, if he asks you to give an example of a project that you did at work, be sure not to give an example of a project you did at school.

- If unsure of the question, ask for clarification.

- If you do not meet all of the job qualifications, give short answers to those questions. Bring the question back to your strengths and the main points you want to make (e.g. I am familiar with web content management tools, but I have not used them in any of my internships, although I used social media tools very successfully). Follow with a quick C.A.R. story that demonstrates that you are a fast learner.

- At the end of the conversation, mention important qualifications that may not have been touched upon. They may very well have been contained in your cover letter, but your cover letter may not have been read, "It's not in resume, but I think it's important to mention that growing up on a farm will help me be successful in a marketing position working with clients and data in the agriculture industry."

- **Mention something that makes you memorable.** This might be a special work or extracurricular achievement or a memorable hobby. You are not there to simply answer questions. SHOW YOUR PERSONALITY (e.g. likeable, charming, funny), and build a clear case for why you should be hired among all candidates. At the end of a day of interviewing several candidates, only the ones who have stood out, will be remembered. Be one of them! "Ping Huang? I remember him well. He was the young man who interned at the mayor's office. When we spoke about his interest in table tennis, I was impressed by his competitiveness."

- At the end of the interview, be clear that you want the job, and end by thanking the interviewer for the opportunity.

After the Interview

As soon as the interview is over, go back to the original coffee shop or other nearby location to write down what you think went well during every stage of the interview, and what you can improve for the next interview. Keep in mind that if the interview did not go well, it may not be due to anything you said or did. Once you think it over, you might decide that you were not really interested in the job or the company.

You can use the following check list to evaluate how you did, and take notes on how to improve for the next interview:

My Non-Verbal Communication

_ I maintained eye contact

_ I used positive body language

_ I consistently showed enthusiasm and energy

_ I did not fidget or otherwise show nervousness

_ I was appropriately dressed

My Verbal Communication

_ I avoided filler words such as Umm

_ I spoke slowly and provided clear responses to questions

_ I emphasized my strengths and highlighted my top skills

_ I used proper grammar and avoided using acronyms

_ I provided specific examples of my accomplishments and strengths with C.A.R. stories

_ I paused to organize my thoughts prior to responding to difficult questions

_ I kept all of my answers under 2 minutes

Also

_ I remained positive throughout

_ I showed self-confidence

_ I expressed well defined career goals

_ I showed my personality (e.g. likeable, charming, funny)

_ I had good chemistry with the interviewer

_ My answers were consistent

_ I finished strong (summarized my case, expressed my enthusiasm for the job and the company, and sold myself as an outstanding candidate)

_ I demonstrated that I researched the organization

_ I asked good questions at the end including asking about next steps

For my next interview, I should focus on improving:

1.

2.

3.

Following Up With a Thank You Note in Writing

A hand-written thank you note on good stationery is optional after an interview, but a thank you email should always be sent for the simple reason that a hand-written note will not allow you to write everything that needs to be communicated:

- Your enthusiasm for the company and job
- Points that you wish you had made (if any)
- Your knowledge of the company and at least one contribution you can make
- Your past successes that align with the company's challenges or goals
- Work samples (if very relevant to your conversation)
- Contact information for your references (but only if requested)
- If following up to a telephone or Skype interview, be sure to mention that you look forward to meeting the interviewer in person.

Send your thank you email within 24 hours. I recommend you write it as soon as you return home from the interview, but don't send it until the following morning. Your brain will continue working on the note even while you sleep, and you are sure to improve it if you take some time between your draft and the final version. Proofread it multiple times before sending it to make sure that your English grammar and spelling are correct and that you are not using American slang. If you are not totally confident in your English grammar, keep your note short, and make an effort to have someone with excellent written English skills quickly proofread and edit it.

Address the interviewer by the same name you used at the interview (e.g. Steven or Mr. Steinfeld), followed by three relatively short paragraphs.

The first paragraph should include the job title and thank him for his time. You might continue by remarking on an interesting exchange that you had during the interview to help him remember how much he liked you. If there is something important that you wish you had pointed out during the interview, you can also mention it at the end of this first paragraph, "By the way, after the interview, I realized that I should have mentioned the fact that I will complete Advanced Excel training next week."

The second paragraph should remind the interviewer why you believe that you are a strong candidate. Be sure to connect your potential contribution with information about the company's immediate needs or longer term challenges or goals.

The last paragraph should talk about your enthusiasm for the opportunity, and indicate when and how you are going to follow up.

Subj: Thank You

Hello Mr Steinfeld,

Thank you for taking the time to interview me yesterday for the position of Marketing Associate. I enjoyed our conversation, particularly the part where we discussed how social media marketing has been exploding over the last few years.

I would like to take this opportunity to highlight a few points that I believe make me a very strong candidate:

---

1. I know what it takes to effectively lead all aspects of weekly retail sales reporting. In my internship at ABC company, I developed multiple sales performance reports to measure the effectiveness of the company's marketing strategies.

2. You mentioned the importance of data analysis. This is one of my greatest skills. When the team at ABC.com needed to assess its publishing partners, I created the new Excel models that were needed to analyze the data from LinkShare.

3. You also mentioned competitive snapshots and pricing assessments. I have conducted competitive analysis and price point comparison projects in each of my internships. I have attached a non-confidential work sample for you to review.

As discussed, I will follow up with you for a status next week. In the interim, please feel free to contact me if you need additional information.

Thank you again for considering me for this opportunity. I am very excited about the possibility of joining your team.

Sincerely.

Vivien Zhu

If you were at a panel interview (several of them and one of you), write the thank you to the person who will be your direct supervisor and copy (.cc) everyone else who was there. If there were multiple but separate interviews, you can do the same, or write a note to each interviewer. If you decide to write separate notes, they should all be slightly different. For example, you might change the sentence where you talk about an interesting exchange you had during the interview.

Following Up by Phone

Although an email is standard practice, you can leave a thank you phone message instead if you are uncomfortable with your writing ability and have no one to review and edit your note. Leave a very short and upbeat message <u>after hours</u> expressing thanks for the time spent interviewing you, and how much you are looking forward to taking the next step. You have only 30 seconds to leave this message, but that should not be a problem. In any event, write down and practice what you are going to say until you can comfortably deliver the message without sounding as if you are reading it. Time the length of your call so that you are not concerned that you may exceed 30 seconds. **Talk very slowly and clearly**. If you make a mistake, opt out of voicemail and re-record the message until you are satisfied. Remember to leave a number where you can be reached at the end of the call.

Hello Mr. Steinfeld, This is Vivian Zhu. I am calling to thank you for taking the time to interview me yesterday. I am very excited about the opportunity, and am looking forward to taking the next step. I can be reached at 888-888-8888. Thank you again.

Decision Day

If you were told that there would be a decision on a certain day ("We will be making a decision by Monday"), assume that you will get their decision within a few days of that date. If you don't hear from him after ten days from the promised decision date (or from the interview date if there was no decision date given), send a friendly email without mentioning that they are beyond the promised decision date.

Subj: Marketing Analyst Interview

Hello Mr. Steinfeld,

Thank you again for the time you spent interviewing me for a Marketing Analyst position ten days ago. I am writing to find out the status of your decision and to let you know of my continued interest and enthusiasm for both the position and the company.

If I do not hear from you soon, I will assume that the position has been filled. If that is the case, I hope that you will consider me for a similar position in the near future.

I look forward to hearing from you soon.

Thank you.

Vivian Zhu

If you still do not hear from them, they may have offered the job to another candidate. If that is the case, you may hear from them if they can't come to terms with that person. In any event, stalking them for an answer will only make you seem desperate, and desperate candidates don't get hired. Trust that they have not forgotten about you. Common courtesy says that they should inform you that you have not been selected, but you may never be notified. **While you are waiting for a decision—even if you feel confident that we will be receiving a job offer—do not slow down your job searching activities.** Always assume that you have not been selected, and keep moving on to new opportunities.

Q. How do I find out why I didn't get the job?

A. You probably don't find out since the company has nothing to gain by sharing that information. There are many good reasons that you were not selected even if you were an outstanding candidate, so **while it is normal to be disappointed, there is no reason to get discouraged.** It might have been as simple as you were not available to start as soon as needed by the employer. Here are some other possibilities:

Why You Were Not Offered the Job

1. There was a more attractive candidate — maybe someone who may not have been as talented as you, but was better able to sell himself, or came highly recommended (a good possibility).

2. The person who got the job was seen as equal or slightly lesser to you, but did not need a work visa. <u>This is why you need to sell yourself as a truly outstanding candidate with a hard to find set of skills and strengths.</u>

3. You did not have excellent chemistry with the interviewer.

4. Someone who did not meet with you made the final decision.

5. You said something on the way out that was a turn-off to the interviewer. Don't let your guard down for a second until after you leave the building.

6. At least one of your references did not give you a strong recommendation.

7. LinkedIn, Facebook, or Google gave negative information about you or did not match with what you said on your resume or at your interview.

8. You did not show enough enthusiasm for the company or the job.

9. You need more interviewing practice.

10. You brought up sponsorship or other visa issues without being asked.

Q. I might not have gotten the job, but how do I know if I did well on the interview?
A. Ask yourself if the interviewer seemed genuinely interested in your answers and was selling you on the company during the interview. If he wasn't, the interview probably did not go as well as you thought. The same is true for the amount of time spent in the interview. Even if the interview does not go well, you will probably be given about 15 minutes to make your case. The more time beyond those 15 minutes, the better it probably went.

Q. What should I do if I get a rejection letter or email?
A. Send a return email thanking the interviewer for his time and consideration of your candidacy. Indicate that you are enthusiastic about working for the company, and would be interested in future opportunities.

Before leaving this chapter, I would like to make one final note about interviewing. **Never turn down a phone or any other type of interview since it will be great practice for when it matters.** In addition, there are 3 other great reasons to interview whenever you can:

1. If you do very well on the interview, you may also be offered a better job than the one for which you are interviewing.

2. It may give you some bargaining power during another interview if you are asked if you are interviewing elsewhere.

3. While the company is interviewing you, you are also interviewing the company. The more you interview, the easier it will be for you to evaluate other companies and opportunities.

Interning Your Way to a Job

"Everybody has to start somewhere. You have your whole future ahead of you. Perfection doesn't happen right away."

–Haruki Murakami, Japanese Author

An internship can be full or part-time, and paid or unpaid depending on the employer and the career field. You will enhance your job prospects greatly if you can get a paid internship—but even if you are not paid; an internship offers the benefit of hands-on-learning and the potential to give you an edge over students without internships.

An internship can also provide you with important networking introductions and references needed to identify and land a job after graduation; and you may even be lucky enough to be mentored by executives, have the opportunity to input ideas to a project team, or present to a group of senior-level managers. If you cannot get a traditional internship, consider alternatives in order to gain experience. For example, if you are a finance student, try for a summer job at a financial advisor's office if you can't land a job at a major investment firm.

While most of the largest corporations recruit for summer internships as early as the fall semester, smaller businesses often

don't start to hire until the spring, so plan accordingly. You can search for internships through online job boards (e.g. www.looksharp. com and www.internships.com) or reach out directly to organizations that interest you without a job posting, but it's important to know that a large number of organizations prefer to find their interns through campus events, often using job fairs and on-campus interviews to identify candidates.

As with all jobs, one of the most successful ways to land an internship is through a strong referral by a trusted employee or other ally of the hiring manager. When you contact that person, send him a note similar to the one below. He may respond to you directly or he may refer your email and resume to the person who recruits interns.

Subj: Internship

Hello Mr. Steinfeld,

I have been researching your company, and came across your name and contact information. I have a strong passion for the media industry. I am hoping that **ABC Company** is willing to consider me for an internship this summer, and would appreciate it if you would meet with me to give me some information and advice or direct my resume to the appropriate person. I believe that I can make a contribution to the company by utilizing my analytical and organizational skills as well as my knowledge and experience in marketing, social media, and event planning.

I look forward to hearing from you. I can be reached at 888- 888-8888. Please find my resume attached.

Thank you for your consideration.

Sincerely,

Vivian Zhu

www.linkedin.com/in/ziyavivzhu

Once you land that internship, think of the internship as a several-week long interview, and work very hard to demonstrate that you have the strengths and skills that will make you a valuable addition to the company when you graduate. However, before you accept any internship, make sure that you will have significant job duties that result in achievement and learning.

Even if the internship is short-term and not renewed under CPT or OPT, continue to stay in touch with your supervisor and co-workers, and check job postings at the company in the months before you graduate. If there is a good match, contact your former supervisor to express your interest in rejoining the company and to discuss the job posting. Even if there is no job posting, contact your former supervisor prior to graduation to discuss anticipated job openings that have not yet been posted. As a known commodity to the company, you pose a low hiring risk, and there is an excellent chance that they will make you a job offer.

Even after graduation, you may want to take advantage of an internship. There is a common misconception that internships are only for college students. Internships are for anyone who has some knowledge in his field but lacks the relevant hands-on experience that employers want to see before they offer a regular full-time position. For example, Wen Huang, a Chinese international student, graduated with a MS degree in Finance. When she did not have a job offer four months after graduation, Wen decided to get some more experience in the U.S. banking industry before returning to China. She applied for, and was given, an unpaid internship in a small bank that had never hired an international student in the past. Even though many of the tasks she was initially given were very basic (e.g. making copies or scanning and archiving documents), her competency and positive attitude did not go unnoticed, and she was soon given more responsibility. To her surprise, after doing a great job in the first few months of her internship, she was offered a full-time position with a very competitive salary and an offer of H-1B sponsorship.

Another international student told me during a mock interview that she entered into her post-graduation summer internship with the understanding that she had only limited time to show what she could contribute to the company. For this reason, she looked for problem solving opportunities. She soon found one when she noticed that the company's three business units were in conflict over the allocation of IT costs. She asked her supervisor if she could use her analytical skills to build a model that might settle these disputes by more fairly and equitably distributing these costs. He said yes, and the end result was that she was offered a full-time position and H-1B sponsorship only weeks after starting the internship.

Internship Interview with Ismail

The following is an interview with Ismail, a career services intern and community services fellow at the Career Transitions Center of Chicago who was particularly successful in landing internship opportunities. Today, he is a Human Capital Consultant at a Big Four company.

Ismail's Background (in his own words):

I am the first person in my family to attain a college degree (as well as my Master's). Each of my two internship searches only took approximately one month to complete successfully. I applied for eight different internships and received offers at five of them. Each interview process was different, but the number of interviews ranged from just one interview up to five interviews before I found out if I would receive an offer. During this process I had roughly 20 to 25 total interviews.

My strategy from the beginning was to talk to people about which companies offer good internships. After I got leads and tips, I began researching each company's industry and its particular products and services. My research included the company's website and social media (LinkedIn, Indeed, and Twitter) to see if the company had a job posting for an internship.

Initially, I applied for internships but did not network. However, I quickly learned that if I wanted to be successful, I needed to network with people inside the company where I wanted to work. If I was not connected with somebody directly working at the company, I looked at my connections on LinkedIn to find out if I had a connection that knew somebody working at the company. If so, I asked to be introduced to the individual for an informational interview, which is a type of interview where you gather information on the company and ask for a referral to the hiring manager if you are still interested in the company after the informational interview. This way, I often had someone hand my resume directly to the hiring manager (and/or recruiter) almost guaranteeing an interview. When I went on an informational interview, I was always sure to do my research on the company and the person I was meeting as well as preparing good questions to ask about his experiences, his company and his industry. I also always had an agenda when going into an informational interview (e.g. networking, getting a referral and/or learning about the company or industry.)

Discovery Step:

Steven: How did you pinpoint the best internships for you?
Ismail: Through due diligence of research and informational interviewing. When I conducted research I tried to learn as much as possible about the company and its industry/services and the internship position (e.g. the different types of learning experiences, roles and responsibilities, exposure to different projects, resources, duration of the internship, and future employment opportunities).

Steven: Did you brainstorm a reasonable number of internships and then research them?

Ismail: I brainstormed a number of times to figure out what I valued most out of an internship. From that point, I created an Excel spreadsheet that would allow me to compare the similarities and differences of potential internships. After comparing and contrasting the internships, I knew where to focus most of my job search energy.

Preparation Step

Steven: Were your internship goals, clear, specific, attainable, realistic, and in writing?
Ismail: At first my goals were not very specific as I was open to all internships. I also thought I could get any internship I wanted without having to put in the extra effort of networking and research. However, once I started doing more research and informational interviewing, my internship goals became more specific and clear. I learned who I needed to network with and which companies to research in-depth. The more engaged I became in the job search process, the more attainable and realistic it became for me to achieve my internship goals.

Steven: Were you organized with weekly goals and a networking log?
Ismail: I did create a weekly goals and a networking log. My weekly goals ranged from having 3 to 5 informational interviews per week, applying to at least two internships, and reading at least 3 articles that would help further my career and brand. The networking log allowed me to track who I talked to, who I should follow up with, where I applied, and if I was referred for a specific internship.

Steven: Did your resume get across what you needed to highlight for the internships you were targeting?
Ismail: My first crack at my resume was way below par and had too much white space on the paper. I had to ask for help to better communicate my

experiences and skills as well as how it was structured. I had several working professionals look at my resume, of course including you. After the feedback and advice I made the necessary changes and my resume began to resonate with individuals. It was also important to learn from my mentors that I should tailor each resume to each position I was planning on applying to.

Steven: Did you take full advantage of networking opportunities? If so, how? If not, why not? What did you learn most in terms of being prepared for interviews?

Ismail: I did take full advantage of networking opportunities by making sure I did research on the individuals I would be networking with. I also made sure I always had an agenda and plan for what I would like to achieve for each networking opportunity whether it was an informational interview or networking event. If it was an informational interview, I always had five to eight questions prepared and no more. The reason is most people tend to talk longer than you expect, so you need wiggle room to ask follow up questions within the 20 to 30 minutes that most people give you.

Action Step

Steven: Did you make a serious time commitment to your internship search? Did you waste time? If yes, how could you have avoided doing so?

Ismail: I put serious attention on my internship search because I wanted the experience and I needed two different internships of 300+ hours to graduate. During the process I allocated time each day into my schedule to do research or network with individuals. I never wasted a minute because you are not the only student fighting for an internship and you never know what that other student is doing to beat you out.

Steven: Did you underestimate the value of networking or informational interviews?

Ismail: At first I underestimated the value of networking since I didn't understand the impact it can have for helping you get a foot in the door. I also learned that the stronger the referral the more likely you are to receive an offer for the internship.

Steven: Did you start early enough? Did you become more proactive over time?

Ismail: I did start early because I knew everybody else in my program was going to be looking for an internship. I wanted to make sure I stayed in front of them in the internship search. Plus they say the early bird gets the worm, meaning the earlier you apply the more likely you will receive an interview and serious consideration. As time went on I became more and more proactive because I learned the importance of networking and research.

Steven: Did you network strategically? How important was LinkedIn?

Ismail: At first I didn't network strategically since I was trying to network with everybody I knew. However, once I realized what type of internship and company I wanted to work for, I began networking strategically. I focused my networking on people who I knew were working at the company or people who knew people outside of my network working at the company.

Steven: Did you make a point of getting to the hiring manager directly?

Ismail: I did not put as much emphasis of getting to the hiring manager as I would have liked. I focused more on networking into the company. If I was able to connect with the hiring manager through my connections, even better! I never asked to talk to the hiring manager unless someone recommended it or offered to get me in touch with him. Usually if the informational interview went well, the interviewer recommended other people to connect with or offered to pass my resume along to the hiring manager and/or recruiter. If the interviewer offered to let me choose who I would like to connect with from his or her list of connections, I asked to be introduced to the hiring manager.

Steven: Did you get out of your comfort zone?
Ismail: I am a confident and authentic individual so I never felt out of my comfort zone. I knew what I wanted and went after it and never gave up. However, I do know people who get very uncomfortable networking and interviewing.

Steven: In summary, what would you say are the keys to landing an internship?
Ismail: I think that the keys to a successful internship search are:

- Doing as much research as possible on the interviewer, the company, and the position
- Having a plan and an agenda for your goals
- Preparing questions to ask
- Practicing answering interview questions
- Networking!
- Having a strong personal identity (understanding your strengths and weaknesses)
- Being authentic during your informational and internship interviews

Volunteer or Part-Time Your Way to a Job

"The best way to find yourself is to lose yourself in the service of others"

– Mahatma Gandhi

Volunteering

Since there are no work authorizations necessary, volunteering can start as soon as your freshman year—but no matter when you start— **volunteer strategically**. If dogs are your passion, and you are pursuing a marketing career, don't volunteer to clean cages at the local pet shelter, volunteer to help with their promotional or event planning activities. Check out websites such as www.volunteermatch.org to find assignments that match you interests, career goals, and time availability.

There are at least seven great reasons to volunteer:

1. It provides one of the easiest and fastest ways to understand the U.S. work culture.

2. It helps improve your English language skills.

3. It gives you the chance to gain experience, sharpen your skills, and learn new skills.

4. Community service work looks impressive on your resume, particularly if demonstrates important strengths such as collaboration, leadership, or program management.

5. Volunteering provides a great opportunity to network. In a nonprofit environment, you not only have the chance to mix with volunteers, but you may have the opportunity to network with staff, the Board of Directors, and corporate donors. You may also have the opportunity to meet important contacts at non-profit social events (you can offer to work as a volunteer at these events even if you have never volunteered at the organization in the past).

6. Volunteering helps build confidence and sense of community that contribute toward maintaining a positive mindset during a sometimes frustrating job search.

7. If your goal is to pursue a non-profit job, it will give you the credentials and understanding of the non-profit culture required to be considered for employment.

When selecting volunteer assignments to pursue, you should know that as an international student, it is very important to avoid volunteer activity that can be seen as unauthorized employment. If you follow the four guidelines below, you should be fine, but check with your international student advisor if you are unsure.

1. You are volunteering for a civic, charitable or humanitarian organization.

2. Your volunteer work is totally voluntary with no direct or indirect pressure by the employer, promise of advancement, or penalty for not volunteering.

3. You are not taking a job that would otherwise be performed by a regular, paid employee.

4. You are not receiving or expecting compensation now or in the future.

Part–Time Work

In addition to earning some money, a qualified part-time job in your field of study can give you many of the same benefits as volunteering, as well as the following:

1. Real world and U.S. business experience in your field

2. Industry or job specific experience to add to your resume

3. Insight into specific industries, companies, or job(s) to pursue in the future

4. The opportunity to network with professionals who can give you referrals and recommendations

5. The ability to stay in the U.S. post-graduation (under OPT regulations).

6. The possibility that it may lead directly to an internship or a full-time job offer (with or without H-1B sponsorship) after graduation

3rd Parties and References

"Depend on yourself and you will never be let down."
– Madhuri Dixit- Indian Bollywood Actress

3rd Party Recruiters

When I say 3rd parties, I am referring to recruiters who do not work directly for an employer. These recruiters, who you might find on LinkedIn or other social media (or they might find you), typically work on a "contingency" basis. This means that they seek out job candidates for their client companies, but they receive no payment from these companies unless their candidates are hired.

Relationships with 3rd party recruiters may expand your opportunities, particularly for STEM related contract positions, but DO NOT DEPEND on them. One reason is that they are usually interested in finding experienced candidates, particularly those who are currently employed (passive candidates). Above all, if you are contacted by a 3rd

party recruiter, please keep in mind that all 3rd party recruiters work only for their clients. <u>Their job is not to help you find a job!</u>

References

Before making the job offer, a company may ask for personal and professional references. <u>You will need to control these references by getting to them before the employer and suggesting to them what they might say if they are called.</u> You will want them to reinforce the skills, strengths, knowledge and experience that the employer showed the most interest in when he interviewed you. When contacting your references, give them a job description, and offer to email them a copy of the job posting.

Hi Steven, I am sending this email to let you know that I gave you as a reference to **ABC Company** for a job as an entry level Financial Analyst. They were very interested in my data analysis skills, so if you would praise my capabilities in that area when they contact you, it might be especially helpful.

Thanks for your help.

Best Regards,

Vivian

If the employer asks for a letter of reference, you can write one for one of your best references to sign if he requests that you do so. If necessary, you can give him a reference letter such as the one below as a sample.

Reference Letter Sample

Dear Mr. Jones,

It is my pleasure to recommend Ziya (Vivian) Zhu. Her performance working as an international marketing intern for ABC Company proved to me that she would be a valuable addition to any company.

I was Vivian's direct supervisor during her summer internship. She worked for me on various projects, including weekly web analytics and marketing performance reporting, and an affiliate marketing program. The quality of her work exceeded our expectations.

I was also greatly impressed by Vivian's contribution to the team. When the team needed to determine an affiliate marketing strategy, she volunteered to help create a LinkShare report analysis; and with her background and knowledge of the Chinese market, she contributed very helpful insights and suggestions in her final internship presentation.

If I can be of any further assistance, or provide you with any further information, please do not hesitate to contact me at steven@abccompany.com.

Sincerely,
Steven Steinfeld
Digital Marketing Manager
ABC Company

When giving a reference, be sure to include the reference's name, position, company, location, phone number, relationship to you (avoid giving family members as references), and background information.

Negotiating Your Salary

"Negotiation assumes parties are more anxious to agree than to disagree."

– Dean Acheson, Former U.S. Secretary of State

International students are usually happy to get any job offer and often accept the salary and other compensation without negotiating. While this is understandable, you should try to negotiate if you need more money to meet your expenses or you feel the offer is unfair. Accepting a lower salary than you think is fair may leave you feeling undervalued and could affect your ability to do your best work — and doing your best work is especially important if you are seeking H-1B sponsorship.

While not immediately accepting the first salary offer may make you uncomfortable, you should know that <u>a "little" negotiation is not unexpected or viewed negatively.</u>

At the Beginning of the Interview Process

Some companies demand a salary history with an online application. Although I do not recommend spending time on online applications unless absolutely necessary; if you do fill out an online application, be honest about your past salary history, but explain during the interview process that your last internship or job is not comparable to the job that you are applying for now.

Many companies may ask the salary question in an initial phone interview. In these early stages, they are not negotiating; they are trying to screen you out. They do not want to waste their time if you expect a salary above their established salary range.

Until the end of the interview process, try to avoid giving a direct answer. Always stress that compensation is important, but not the most important factor in applying for or accepting the job. Say that you are "flexible" or "open," or "I am interested in finding a job that is a good fit for me. I'm sure whatever salary you're paying is within the established salary range for the job." If they insist on an answer, give a very wide-range based upon your research, with your minimum acceptable salary number at the bottom of the range. For example, if you have researched a job that has a salary range of $40,000-$50,000, but the minimum that you will accept is $42,000, say, "Based upon my research, my understanding is that the range for this job is $42,000-$50,000. I am comfortable in that range." If they don't show concern with your answer, you know that your salary will not be a big issue.

Understanding the Salary Range

If the salary range is not listed on the job description, there are several websites (salary.com, payscale.com, bls.gov, NACE salary calculator, jobstar.org, glassdoor.com, vault.com, indeed.com) that can give you an idea of salary trends and the salary range for a specific job in a specific industry in a specific geography. You should check at least two of these sites BEFORE your first interview. It's important to know the range for the job because if you don't know the established range, you may mention a number that is too high and be screened out. If you give a number that is too low, you will likely get a lower amount than you might otherwise be offered. Keep in mind that large employers extend offers of salary based upon their company's established range for the position that may or may not be an exact match with your research.

At the End of the Interview Process

When they have determined that you are their number one candidate, they may tell you the salary that they have in mind, or they may ask you what you expect to receive. If they ask you for a number, say, "I'd appreciate it if you would make me an offer based on whatever you have budgeted for this position," since they may offer you more than you might expect.

If you want the job, but the company they offer you less than you need or expected, ask politely about other ways to reach your salary goal; "I would love to work here, but I was hoping for a little higher salary. Would it be possible to raise the salary by 10%?" If they say "no," ask if you can have a salary review in three months if you do an outstanding job.

It's important to remember that if you are being offered the job, you are their first choice, and they may improve their offer rather than risk losing you. Just be sure to keep the conversation very friendly, and do not ask for more than 10% more than they originally offered unless you need more to pay your bills.

Small to mid-sized companies will typically be more flexible in negotiating with you than a large company. Whatever the size of the company, you will be almost guaranteed to receive a better offer, and greater negotiating power, if you have exceptional technical skills, great chemistry with the hiring manager, and/or come to the company by way of a referral with a strong recommendation and glowing references.

Before Accepting the Job

Take a step back to look at the whole picture. Even if you are happy with compensation, benefits, or vacation time, there are many other important considerations. Ask yourself the following questions:

1. Am I happy with the job responsibilities?

2. Can I live with the reputation and culture of the organization and the reputation of my new boss?

3. Does this job fit with my short and long term career goals?

4. Am I happy with how the job title will look on my resume? (If not happy, ask for a job title you feel will look better on your resume).

5. Can I live with the job location, lack of public transportation, required living expenses, or amount of travel time to and from work?

6. Is there a good chance that they will sponsor me for an H-1B visa if I do an outstanding job?

The list goes on and on… Get the answers to ALL of your important questions BEFORE you accept the offer.

If you are satisfied, ask for the offer stating the salary, benefits, and firm start date in writing

Job Search and Mindset

"Change your thoughts and you change your world."

— Norman Vincent Peale- American Minister and Author of "The Power of Positive Thinking"

A successful job search does not start by looking outward for new opportunities. It starts with looking inward at your current level of fear, anxiety, and motivation. No matter how strong your resume or skill set, without a positive mindset, you will be challenged to put the needed focus, energy, and confidence into successfully implementing and sustaining the 3-step job search approach.

Although you may be feeling more comfortable with your English skills and cultural knowledge, you may have times when you feel insecure or uncertain. You may also worry about the limited time you have available to find an internship before the summer or a sponsored job before your visa expires. The urgency that you feel can easily turn into panic or general emotional distress that will slow down or stop your job search unless you know how to handle feeling of frustration and rejection. The job search period could last for at least a few months. **If you stay confident, strong, positive, patient and determined, and follow the guidance offered in this book, success will come.**

Mindset includes beliefs and assumptions that lead us to making certain decisions. Sometimes these are self-defeating. For example, if you assume that a company does not hire international students based solely upon what another person told you, you are unlikely to contact that company. On the other hand, it you believe that every company is open to hiring international students, you have a good chance of changing your experience and your outcome. This is one reason that I advise international students to apply to any organization that does not specifically state that they exclude foreign nationals. The worst you can receive is a polite rejection.

The best way to develop and sustain a positive job search mindset is by pursuing jobs where you feel you are an excellent fit. You will know that you are an excellent fit when you start getting interviews that are of great interest to you. Unfortunately, sometimes a job seeker will get many interviews, and do relatively well at them, but totally change course or give up out of frustration. Don't fall into this trap! Continue to improve your interviewing skills, and you will jump to number one.

Tips for Improving Mindset

- Understand that setbacks are normal. Stay organized and committed to follow your job search plan.

- Remember that getting better at something (like job search) requires practice, patience and persistence.

- Seek out positive-thinking friends who are also looking for jobs, and support each other. Stay away from anyone with a negative mindset, especially other international students who have low expectations or have given up job searching in the U.S.

- Start the day with quiet time to get in touch with your frame of mind and energy level. You might want to practice meditation, tai chi, or yoga during this time, and follow quiet time with some upbeat motivational or inspirational music.

- Take a slow walk or a long shower, or even daydream, during the day to stir creative and constructive ideas.

- Combat stress. Focus on physical and emotional health with a good amount of sleep, exercise and nutrition (especially mood enhancing foods such as tomatoes, fatty fish, dark chocolate, and peppermint tea), and visualization. Taking even five or six slow deep breaths with your eyes closed can help a lot when you feel stressed.

- Pursue things that you love to do. Do at least one thing every day that makes you happy. This does not need to take a long time.

- Get involved in extra-curricular activities (e.g. school play, sports, volunteering). This will improve your confidence level, and may also help you to expand your network of American friends.

- Spend time in your local community (e.g. working out of the local Starbucks). Engage with Americans to practice your English with small talk, and you might expand your network of American friends or professional network contacts and increase your confidence.

- Learn a little more about U.S. culture every day (e.g. TV, movies, music, blogs, and video games).

- Have the courage to ask people for a favor, an introduction, an interview, or a phone call on your behalf. Remember the courage that allowed you to come to study and work in a country with a very different language and culture.

Visa Laws and Your Work Options

Co-Authored by Ron Cushing, Director of International Services at the University of Cincinnati

Please always check information in this chapter with government or academic authorities for applicability to your personal situation and to be certain that there have been no recent changes. There is a list of online resources at the end of this chapter to also help in that process.

The Immigration and Nationality Act provides that international students must be coming to the United States solely to pursue a full-course of academic, language, or other non-vocational study. Nevertheless, F-1, M-1 and J-1 international students may work under certain circumstances. Department of Homeland Security (DHS) regulations define "employment" as services or labor for wages or other remuneration.

International student employment can be divided into three distinct categories: on-campus, academic/practical training, and off-campus. It is important for students to understand the U.S. immigration process when having discussions with prospective employers. Students can't assume that employers understand immigration laws or know what approvals are necessary to prove employment eligibility. Knowing what you can and can't do could be the difference in whether or not you get hired or maintain proper immigration status in the U.S.

This chapter discusses questions frequently asked by employers about hiring international students, the various employment authorizations students may obtain, and the common types of employment visas to which international students will transition once their student work authorizations have been exhausted.

Definition of Important Terms

It's important to understand the terms, agencies and immigration classifications associated with international student employment that will be discuss in this chapter. This is not an exhaustive list, but it should provide a very good overview.

Department of Homeland Security (DHS)

The Department of Homeland Security is a cabinet level department responsible for securing the nation's borders and managing the immigration process. DHS assumes responsibilities for activities and services previously handled by the Immigration and Naturalization Service. The DHS has divided immigration services and border enforcement into separate agencies.

U.S. Citizenship and Immigration Services (CIS)

An agency within the Department of Homeland Security with jurisdiction over the status of nonimmigrants within the boundaries of the U.S. This agency has direct oversight of immigration related benefits including change of status, employment authorization, etc.

U.S. Department of State (DOS)

The government agency responsible for issuing U.S. visas. This agency is also responsible for oversight of the J-1 Exchange Visitor Program, including waivers of the two year home residency requirement.

Department of Labor (DOL)

The Department of Labor is the government agency with oversight of U.S. labor laws. The DOL has direct authority over H-1B Specialty Worker laws.

Internal Revenue Service (IRS)

The Internal Revenue Service (IRS) is the U.S. government agency that collects taxes. The IRS issues various forms (withholding allowance certificates, income tax returns, etc.) which are used to help international visitors pay the taxes that apply to them. The IRS also determines how much an individual owes in taxes, and whether an organization that pays income to an international visitor is required to withhold specific amounts from that income.

U.S. Immigration and Customs Enforcement (ICE)

An Agency within the Department of Homeland Security with jurisdiction over immigration enforcement issues. This is the agency with direct oversight of the Student and Exchange Visitor Information System (SEVIS) program. SEVIS is an electronic reporting and record-keeping system for nonimmigrant students (F-1 and M-1) and exchange visitors (J-1). SEVIS has direct connections to ICE officers and U.S. embassies and consulates abroad. SEVIS requires schools and exchange visitor programs to record on an "events-based" schedule, I-20 and DS-2019 issuance, work recommendations and authorizations, student violations, etc.

Employment Authorization Document

Certain international visitors authorized to work will have an Employment Authorization

Document (EAD). An EAD is a laminated picture I.D. card issued by the CIS authorizing the holder to accept employment. All EAD's have a start and end date. The EAD must be valid for the international visitor to use it for employment verification.

For Curricular Practical Training (CPT), F-1 students receive authorization from the school (NOT from USCIS) on page two of the student's I-20. J-1 students receive work authorization on the DS-2019 form. Typically, a letter is also issued by the RO or ARO at their institution.

E-3 Visa: A work visa classification for Australian nationals admitted to perform services in a specialty occupation.

F-1 Visa: Students studying in colleges, universities, seminaries, conservatories, academic high schools, other academic or language institutions.

H-1B Visa: A work visa classification for foreign nationals admitted to perform services in a specialty occupation.

J-1 Visa: Visitors engaged in educational and cultural exchanges for the purpose of studying, teaching, conducting research or other activities that increase mutual understanding between people of the U.S. & other countries. J-1 students are typically funded by international agencies or the student's home government. In cases where support is being provided by an international agency (Fulbright, LASPAU, etc.) the agency, not the school, will issue the DS-2019.

M-1 Visa: Students studying in vocational or trade schools.

O-1 Visa: A work visa classification for aliens of extraordinary ability in the sciences, arts, education, business or athletics.

TN Visa: A work visa classification for Canadian or Mexican nationals admitted to work under the terms of the North American Free Trade Agreement.

Certificate of Eligibility (form I-20 or DS-2019): International visitors on F-1 or J-1 status will have a certificate of eligibility for nonimmigrant visa status. This certificate may be a Form I-20 for F-1 students or Form DS-2019 for J-1 Exchange visitors. The end date on the I-20 or DS-2019 indicates how long the international visitor is permitted to stay.

General Information for F-1, M-1 and J-1 Students

Most international students are in the U.S. on non-immigrant student visas (F-1, M-1 and J-1), and these international students are eligible to accept employment under certain conditions. It is important for you to understand your work options associated with your status.

On-Campus Employment

International students on F-1 and J-1 immigration status are eligible to work on campus 20 hours per week while school is in session (M-1 students cannot work on-campus). There is no hourly limitation during scheduled breaks. In addition to on-campus employment on the school's premises, the regulations provide for on-campus employment which takes place at an off-campus location "educationally affiliated with the school." F-1 and J-1 students are eligible to begin on-campus employment immediately upon being admitted to the United States in F-1 status. Pursuant to Department of State regulations, this may be as much as 30 days before classes begin. Student simply need to follow the procedures established at the institution for having the employment eligibility (I-9) verified. J-1 students must have their on-campus employment authorized by the Responsible/Alternate Responsible Officer in the SEVIS system.

Off-Campus Employment

In addition to the possibilities for practical training, F-1 and J-1 students may be authorized to work off-campus, but only after having been in F-1 or J-1 status for one academic year, and only after meeting certain criteria. Students who are experiencing unforeseen economic hardship and students who have a job offer from an international organization may apply for work authorization from the DHS. M-1 students are not eligible for these types of off-campus employment.

Practical Training for F-1 and M-1 Students

Practical training is available to F-1 and M-1 students who have been attending a college, university, conservatory, or seminary full time for at least nine consecutive months.

Practical training is divided into two types, "Curricular" and "Optional." Curricular Practical Training (CPT) provides for employment which is an "integral" part of the established curriculum and is usually required or for credit. <u>M-1 students are not eligible for CPT</u>. **Optional Practical Training (OPT)** provides for employment "directly related to the student's major area of study." Students, in general, must have completed one academic year (approximately nine months) in F-1 and M-1 status and must maintain their status to be eligible for practical training.

Curricular Practical Training (CPT) for F-1 Students

Curricular practical training is designed to provide students with an opportunity to gain actual employment experience that is "an integral part of an established curriculum." Such training is defined as "alternate work/ study, internship, cooperative education, or any other type of required internship or practicum which is offered by sponsoring employers through cooperative agreements with the school. Training must be a required or integral part of a program of study."

Another example of curricular practical training would be a graduate student engaged in research that is part of a thesis or dissertation. The research should involve innovative technology available only at a particular corporation's research facilities or to collect data essential for completion of a thesis or dissertation.

In order to obtain employment authorization for curricular practical training students must have completed one academic year in lawful status and currently be in F-1 status. The exception is graduate students who are required to start a co-op or internship prior to completing one academic year study. The Designated School Official (DSO) at the institution completes the employment authorization in SEVIS by indicating the name and location of the employer, the dates of employment, and whether the employment is full-time or part-time. Employment of 20 hours per week or less is part-time. Anything over 20 hours a week is considered full-time.

The student's I-20 form endorsed for CPT, I-94 card and unexpired foreign passport is the employment authorization. No authorization is needed from the Department of Homeland Security.

Students are not limited in the amount of CPT training they may utilize. However, students who have engaged in one year or more of full-time CPT are ineligible for OPT.

OPT for F-1 and M-1 Students

F-1 students are eligible for 12 months of OPT for each higher degree level they obtain. Students who obtain a degree in Science, Technology, Engineering, and Mathematics (STEM) may be eligible for an additional

24 months of OPT. M-1 students are eligible a maximum of 6 months of OPT or 1 month of OPT for every 4 months of study completed.

OPT is an opportunity for F-1 and M-1 students to gain work experience to complement their academic program. All F-1 students are entitled to one year of OPT for each higher degree they receive. Students who complete a degree on STEM Designated Degree Program List may be entitled to a 24-month extension of OPT (36 months total). Students can obtain a second 24 month STEM OPT period if the student obtains a degree at a higher level. M-1 students get one maximum period of 6 months of OPT (or 1 month of OPT for every 4 months of study).

OPT must be authorized by the U.S. Citizenship and Immigration Services (USCIS) based on a recommendation from the designated school official (DSO) at the school which issued the I-20 to the student. Form I-20 is a government document which verifies the student's admission to that institution. Student will receive an Employment Authorization Document (EAD) from the USCIS that establishes their ability to work.

STEM refers to degrees in science, technology, engineering, or mathematics and includes:

Actuarial Science, Computer Science (except data entry/microcomputer applications)

Engineering, Engineering Technologies, Biological and Biomedical Sciences, Mathematics and Statistics, Military Technologies, Physical Sciences, Science Technologies, Medical Scientist.

To qualify for the 24-month STEM extension, the F-1 students' employer must be enrolled in the E-Verify Employment Verification Program operated by U.S. Citizenship and Immigration Services. The student and the employer must submit an I-983 Training Plan for STEM OPT as part of the application process and Students and must submit yearly progress reports signed by the employer to the school DSO. The STEM OPT extension rule also provides the DHS with discretion to conduct employer site visits at worksites to verify whether employers are meeting program requirements, including that they possess and maintain the ability and resources to provide structured and guided work-based learning experiences. DHS will provide notice to the employer 48 hours before any site visit unless a complaint or other evidence of noncompliance with the STEM OPT extension regulations triggers the visit, in which case DHS may conduct the visit without notice.

OPT for F-1 students falls into four categories: (1) during the student's annual vacation and at other times when school is not in session if the student is eligible, and intends to register for the next term or session; (2) while school is in session provided that OPT does not exceed 20 hours a week; (3) full-time after completion of all course requirements for the degree (excluding thesis or the equivalent), if the student is in a bachelor's, master's or doctoral degree program; (4) full-time after completion of a program of study.

OPT for M-1 students can only be authorized after completion of the program of study.

To engage in OPT employment the student must apply for an Employment Authorization Document (EAD) from the DHS center having jurisdiction over their place of residence. This is done with a recommendation through the student's DSO.

OPT employment must be related to the student's field of study. A communication major, for example, is not eligible to work as a computer programmer on OPT. The student may not accept OPT employment until the DHS approves the application and provides the student with an EAD. Employers should be aware that the amount of time it takes the DHS to approve the EAD is beyond the control of the student or the school. Delays of 90 days or more are typical during the summer months.

In order to continue employment at the conclusion of OPT a student would need to have an approved change of status to one of the employment categories (H-1B, TN, J-1, O-1, etc.) or have obtained lawful permanent residence or an EAD authorizing employment.

Unemployment

While on OPT there are limits on how long you can remain in the U.S. while unemployed. For F-1 students on 12-month OPT the maximum amount of time you can remain unemployed is 90 days. F-1 students who qualify for and receive the 24-month OPT extension can be unemployed for an aggregate of 150 days. This particular part of the rule puts responsibility on students to keep their International Services up to date with name and address of your OPT employer. M-1 students are not allowed to remain in the U.S. unemployed while on OPT.

Cap-Gap OPT for F-1 Students

F-1 students who are the beneficiaries of pending or approved H-1B petitions, but whose period of authorized F-1 stay expires before the H-1B employment start date can extend their status AND work authorizations. This rule applies to all students on OPT, not just STEM students. The extension of duration of status and work authorization automatically terminates upon the rejection, denial, or revocation of the H-1B petition filed on the student's behalf. OPT can be extended between April 1st and through September 30th of a given year if the student is the beneficiary of a timely-filed H-1B petition requesting change of status and an employment start date of October 1 of the following H-1B fiscal year. The Cap-Gap OPT is an automatic extension of duration of status and employment authorization to bridge the gap between the OPT end date and start of H-1B status. The automatic extension of OPT is terminated upon the rejection, denial, or revocation of the H-1B petition. The student must obtain a Cap-Gap I-20 authorizing the employment from a DSO at the institution they graduated from.

Academic Training for J-1 Students

International students on J-1 visas are eligible for work authorization called academic training. Students in bachelor's or master's programs can obtain 18 months of Academic Training. Post-doctoral students may apply for additional 18 months of Academic Training. Some J-1 program participants are also allowed to work part-time during the academic program. Academic Training is authorized by the Responsible Officer (RO) or Alternate Responsible Officer (ARO). Students should consult with the RO or ARO at their institution.

Employment With an International Organization for F-1 Students

A special situation exists for F-1 students who have been offered employment under the sponsorship of an international organization, as defined by the International Organization Immunities Act. A student seeking permission to work for such an organization makes application to the DHS Service Center having jurisdiction over his or her residence by submitting the following: 1) a written certification from the organization that the proposed employment is within the scope of the organization's sponsorship, 2) a Form I-20 ID endorsed for employment in SEVIS by the DSO within the last 30 days, and 3) a completed Form I-765, Application for Employment Authorization, with the fee required.

Frequently Asked Questions by Employers About International Student Employment

Below are some commonly asked questions by employers about international student employment. It is important to know the answers to these questions.

Isn't it illegal to hire international students because they do not have a green card?

No. Federal regulations permit the employment of international students on F-1, M-1 and J-1 visas within certain limits. These visas allow students to work in jobs related to their major field of study. F-1 and M-1 students can work on "practical training." J-I students may work on "academic training."

Even if it's legal to hire international students, won't it cost a lot of money and involve a lot of paperwork?

No. The only cost to the employer hiring international students is the time and effort to interview and select the best candidate for the job. The international student office handles the paperwork involved in securing the work authorization for F-1 and J-1 students. In fact, a company may save money by hiring international students because the majority of them are exempt from Social Security (FICA) and Medicare tax requirements.

How long can international students work in the United States with their student visa?

F-1 students who are eligible for Curricular Practical Training (CPT) can work for the amount of time necessary to complete the curricular work requirements. All F-1 students are eligible for an additional 12 months of OPT, either before or following graduation, or a combination of the two. Students who complete a bachelor, master or doctoral degree in a STEM field may work for 24 additional months of OPT (for a total of 36 months of OPT) at an E-Verify employer. However, if they work full-time for one year or more using CPT, they are not eligible for OPT.

M-1 students are not eligible for CPT, but may be eligible for up to 6 months of OPT.

Students with a J-1 visa are usually eligible to work up to 18 months following graduation, three years for post-doctoral work. This type of employer is called Academic Training. J-1 students may also be eligible to work part-time during their program of study. The Responsible Officer (RO) or Alternate Responsible Officer (ARO) will evaluate each student's situation to determine the length of time for which they are eligible to work.

Don't international students need work authorization before I can hire them?

No. International students must have the work authorization before they begin actual employment, but not before they are offered employment. In fact, J-1 students must have a written job offer in order to apply for the work authorization. Many F-1 and M-1 students will be in the process of obtaining work authorization while they are interviewing for employment. Students can give employers a reasonable estimate of when they expect to receive work authorization.

What if I want to continue to employ international students after their work authorization expires?

With a bit of planning ahead, an employer can hire international students to continue to work for them in the H-1B visa category for a total of six years (authorization is granted in two three-year periods). The H-1B is a temporary working visa for workers in a "specialty occupation." The application procedure to the USCIS is straightforward. The job must meet only two basic requirements as of January 2017, but these requirments may change.

1) The salary must meet the prevailing wage as defined by the Department of Labor

2) A bachelor's degree in a specific field is a minimum normal requirement for the position.

Doesn't an employer have to prove that international students are not taking jobs from a qualified American?

No. American employers are not required to document that a citizen of another country did not take a job from a qualified American. Employers must document that they did not turn down a qualified American applicant for the position only when they wish to hire foreign citizens on a permanent basis and sponsor them for permanent resident status ("green card").

Can I hire international students as volunteer interns?

Normally, if the internship involves no form of compensation and is truly voluntary and does not replace a paid position, the students may volunteer without having to do any paperwork with the USCIS or their school. If, however, the internship provides a stipend or any compensation, students must obtain permission for practical training or academic training prior to starting their internship.

What is the cost of E-Verify program and how can I enroll in E-Verify program?

There is no cost to register in E-Verify program. Information on E-verify and the enrollment procedure can be found at the USCIS website at www.uscis.gov/everify.

Continuing Employment after the Practical/Academic Training Period

Federal regulations require that employment terminate at the conclusion of the authorized practical or academic training. However, students on an F-1 or M-1 visa, or students on a J-1 visa who are not subject to a two-year home residency requirement, may continue to be employed if they receive approval for a change in visa category. The most common immigration statuses that allow for work beyond the student visa include: H-1B Specialty Worker; J-1 Exchange Visitor; TN Trade NAFTA (for Canadian and Mexican nationals); E-3 (for Australian Nationals); O-1 Extraordinary Ability.

H-1B Specialty Worker Visas

H-1B specialty workers are international visitors who have skills and experience of a special nature that require at least a bachelor's degree or equivalent combination of education and experience. An applicant is not permitted to begin work for an employer until an H-1B is approved for the employer. There is an exception for individuals who currently hold H-1B status for another employer. H-1B employees have a maximum stay of six (6) years in the category no matter how many different employers they have. Employment can be granted for a maximum of three (3) year increments. Extensions beyond the six year limit are available if an employer has initiated green card efforts prior to the end of the fifth year of H-1B status.

The initial petition for an individual worker can be approved for up to three years. The validity of an H-1B petition is linked to the particular employer, employee, job duties, location and wage. If there are material changes in the terms of employment or the legal identity of the employer during the petition period, the H-1B may be considered automatically invalidated. If the employee engages in work activities not authorized on the petition, the employee is in violation of U.S. laws and potentially deportable. The employer may request an extension for up to an additional three years. However, most foreign workers are subject to a six-year limit in H-1B status. Any time spent working under a previous employer's H-1B petition will count toward the six year limit in H-1B status.

Frequently Asked Questions About the H-1B Process

Is there a quota limiting the number of new H-1B workers?

The government's fiscal year is from October 1 to September 30. Sixty-five thousand (65,000) H-1B petitions can be approved during a fiscal year. Additionally, twenty thousand (20,000) petitions can be approved for individuals who have obtained a Master's degree or higher from a U.S. institution.

Each foreign national (with the three exceptions noted below), who is approved for H-1B classification is counted in this determination. However, approvals for extensions of stay in H-1B classification, sequential employment, concurrent employment, and amended petitions are not counted in this determination.

H-1B employees of higher education institutions, nonprofit research organizations and government research organizations are not counted toward the quota. However, if they change employers to a nonexempt employer, they will be counted toward the quota in the year they changed employers. Furthermore, individuals counted toward the quota in the previous six years of H-1B status who have been outside the United States for one full year and are again seeking admission pursuant to H-1B classification will be counted toward the quota.

Not every H-1B applicant is subject to the cap. Visas will still be available for applicants filing for amendments, extensions, and transfers unless they are transferring from an exempt employer or exempt position and were not counted towards the cap previously. The cap also does not apply to applicants filing H-1B visas through institutions of higher education, nonprofit research organizations, and government research organizations.

How long does it take to get an H-1B petition approved?

Currently, a reasonable window of expectation is about two to three months. Because each H-1B petition revolves around facts related to the individual candidate, as well as to the employer and the position, there is some variation in the preparation and processing time needed for H-1B cases. By paying an extra $1,225 expedited processing fee to U.S. Citizenship and Immigration Services, an employer can anticipate H-1B petition processing within fifteen (15) calendar days and can be filed no earlier than 4 months prior to start date. If the annual quota for new H-1B workers is reached, processing could be delayed until October 1st, when the next fiscal year begins. If the candidate is outside the United States, processing times can be increased by several weeks or months while the U.S. government completes security clearances and consular visa processing.

What are the fees involved in filing an H-1B case?

There are multiple fees involved in filing an H-1B petition. The total amount to be paid depends on whether the petition is a "new" petition and whether the employer is an institution of higher education or a non-profit governmental or research organization.

H-1B Fees:

Base Filing Fee	$325
USCIS Anti Fraud Fee	$500 (Initial Petitions)
ACWIA Education and Training Fee	$750 (For employers less than 25 employees) or $1500 (For employees more than 25 employees)
Public Law 111-320 Fee	$4,000
Premium Processing (Optional)	$1,225

There is currently a $325.00 application fee that is required of all H-1B petitions. A $500.00 fraud prevention and detection fee is required for and employer's "initial" petition. "Initial" petitions include any application by an employer for an employee who currently does not hold H-1B status or for an employee who currently holds H-1B status for another employer.

For employers who are not an institution of higher education or a non-profit governmental or research organization, an additional training fee is required. The fee is $750 for employers with 25 or fewer full-time equivalent employees and $1,500 for employers with 26 or more full-time equivalent employees. H-1B petitioners that employ 50 or more employees in the United States, if more than 50 percent of these employees are in H-1B, L-1A or L-1B status, must pay a $4,000 training fee. There is an optional premium processing fee of $1,225 that can be paid. The premium processing fee guarantees an answer on the petition within 15 days of receipt at the USCIS. Finally, if the employee already in the U.S. has dependents who need H-4 dependent status a fee of $290.00 is required for the I-539 form.

Who usually pays the legal expenses?

As with the filing fee, a Department of Labor regulation generally requires the employer to pay. The regulation states that all costs in connection with preparation and filing of the LCA and H-1B petition are considered the employer's business expenses and must be paid by the employer, and the employer cannot be reimbursed by the employee.

Department of Labor regulations require that the employer pay the H-1B filing fees (application fee, training fee, fraud prevention and detection fee). The optional premium processing fee (paid to obtain faster processing) may in some cases be paid by the employee or a third-party.

Can I add/change employers?

Workers in H-1B status are only allowed to work for a petitioning employer. There is no restriction on changing employers or working for more than one employer concurrently. So long as the new employer follows proper H-1B petitioning procedures, an H-1B employee can add/change employers. Employers hiring workers already in H-1B status under certain circumstances may be allowed to commence the employment upon filing their H-1B petition, rather than waiting for approval.

J-1 Exchange Visitors

J-1 status holders are referred to as exchange visitors. Institutions must be designated as an exchange visitor program in order to issue a DS-2019 for J-1 status. Most major institutions of higher education have such designation as do most governmental agencies (NIH, EPA, etc.). J-1 exchange visitors are limited to work on the premises of the institution that issued the DS-2019. Under certain circumstances some exchange visitors may be authorized to do work, give lectures, or engage in other activities off the premises of the sponsor. Such employment must be specifically authorized in writing by the sponsor. J-1 exchange visitors can fall into one of the following categories: Professor; Research Scholar; Short-Term Scholar; Specialist; Student (degree and non-degree); AuPair; Camp Counselor; Alien Physician; Trainee; Government Visitors; Intern and Summer Work. Each category has its own time limitations. The J-1 visa classification can serve as an excellent option when an H-1B visa is not possible or that time has been exhausted, provided the employer has the appropriate designation from the Department of State.

Two-Year Home Country Physical Presence Requirement

The two-year home country physical presence requirement is one of the most important special characteristics of exchange visitor status and should be thoroughly understood by the student and the employer. An exchange visitor subject to the two year requirement is not eligible to obtain permanent residency, H temporary worker or trainee, or L intra-company transferee status in the United States until they have resided and been physically present in their country of nationality or last legal permanent residence for a total of at least two years following departure from the United States. They are also not permitted to change to another non-immigrant status in the United States.

TN Trade NAFTA

The TN visa classification if for Canadian and Mexican nationals admitted for employment under the terms of the North American Free Trade Agreement (NAFTA). The type of employment must be included on the approved list of occupations and can last up to three years in duration, although the employment can be renewed multiple times. This is a good employment option for Canadian and Mexican nationals when the H-1B cap is reached or the employer doesn't want to pay the expenses associated with an H-1B petition.

Under NAFTA (North American Free Trade Agreement) Canadian/ Mexican professionals may apply to enter the U.S. under the TN visa classification.

List of TN professions can be found at:

http://canada.usembassy.gov/visas/doing-business-in-america/professions-covered-by-nafta.html

E-3 Visas

The E-3 visa classification is designed for Australian nationals. E-3 employees have a maximum stay of two years that can be renewed.

O-1 Alien of Extraordinary Ability

O-1 status is available to persons of extraordinary ability in the sciences, business, athletics, and education. O-1 status is also available to persons of extraordinary ability in the arts, however, the standards are different. O-1 status is an excellent option for persons subject to the two year home residency requirement who are not eligible for H-1B specialty worker status. O-1 applicants must demonstrate that they have made outstanding contributions in their field and they have risen to the top of their field and enjoy sustained national or international acclaim.

Recommended Online Resources

http://www.aila.org (American Immigration Lawyers Association)
www.lawmh.com (Mark B. Rhoads, Immigration Attorney)
http://www.uscis.gov (U.S. Citizenship and Immigration Services)
http://www.myvisajobs.com/ (comprehensive employment and visa portal).
http://www.onedayoneinternship.com/ (internship information and opportunities)
http://www.naceweb.org (National Association of Colleges and Employers)
http://www.youtube.com/channel/HCGHKZycvcIo4 (H-1B topics)
http://www.goinglobal.com/en/guide-detail/?guide_id=27 (U.S. employment information)
http://www.uscis.gov/e-verify

After Landing Your Job in the USA

"To profit from good advice requires more wisdom than to give it"

— Wilson Mizner- American Playwright

When you get that internship, volunteer or part-time assignment, or full-time position, maximize your chances for a better position and/or visa sponsorship by:

1. Finding and fully utilizing mentors inside and outside the organization who can help guide you to success (you may want to have multiple mentors to accomplish different goals).
2. Preparing for performance reviews by documenting your accomplishments.
3. Understanding and supporting your supervisor's short and long term priorities.
4. Being unafraid to ask for whatever tools and help you need to excel at your job.
5. Being confident enough to express your good ideas to management.
6. Seriously considering returning to school to obtain one or more advanced degrees (e.g. Masters, PhD).

7. Whether you are in an internship, temporary OPT assignment, or full-time job—<u>go to work every single day with the goal of proving that you deserve to stay with the company long term.</u>

8. Continually building your LinkedIn professional network.

9. Figuring out what you love to do, and always doing it to the best of your ability!

10. **Engaging your co-workers**. Build strong relationships with everyone in the organization by being polite, friendly, and helpful. You never know who might be in a position to hire or refer you into a better position in the future and/or provide you with an important reference.

    Since networking in the U.S. does not come naturally to most international students, an invitation from your co-workers to join them at the end of the work day may be one of those situations that make you make up an excuse to avoid getting out of your comfort zone. This may be particularly true if you are invited to go to a bar after work, especially if you don't drink alcohol.

    Avoid the temptation to give an excuse and go directly home. In fact, if you see them going out, and they have not thought to invite you to join them; you should ask to join the group ("Would it be okay if I tagged along?" "If you have room, I would be happy to join you").

    Why would you want to get out of your comfort zone to join them? Here are 5 reasons:

    1- They will sense that you are making up an excuse not to join them, especially since you may not have had time to think up a good one. They may think you don't like one or more of them, and may never ask you again.

    2- Even if you just have a Coke, you will be more likely to be seen as part of the team, and will give you a chance to mix with co-workers who can help you problem solve when they are not under pressure to complete their own work.

3- It will help to increase your comfort with U.S. language and culture.

4- Getting out of your comfort zone to mix with your co-workers and allowing them to get to know you on a personal level can lead to important recommendations for a full-time position, H-1B sponsorship or promotion.

5- It can lead to new and unexpected friendships.

Job Search Coaching

"Every great achiever is inspired by a great mentor."
– Lailah Gifty Akita, Ghanian Author

More than any other group of individuals that I coach, international students should consider professional career and job search coaching.

If you started your job search late, or your job search is progressing slowly, hiring a job search coach can turn out to be a fantastic return on investment since the right coach can greatly accelerate and improve your job search results. But since coaches have differing levels of skill, background and experience working with international students, you will need to select a coach wisely. Once you identify a few potential coaches by virtue of reputation or personal recommendation (I hope that Steinfeld Coaching will be one of them), I suggest that you ask each one the following 10 questions to improve you chance of making the best decision.

Q1. How long have you been a job search coach?

Q2. How many international student clients have you had, and what percentage have landed a full-time job?

Q3. Do you have specific knowledge of my field or a closely related field?

Q4. Are you a recognized job search authority (e.g. published author, interviewed in print, radio or TV, popular speaker)? Do you have a relatively high number of LinkedIn Recommendations and Endorsements? (Note: You can also get much of this information from his LinkedIn profile)

Q5. Do you charge by the hour or do you put in whatever time is necessary over a fixed period of time for a fixed fee? (Note: I offer both at Steinfeld Coaching, but fixed fee is usually the best option for international students since they always need more than one-hour per week of networking or interviewing coaching, as well as almost daily help editing written job search correspondence.

Q6. What process and tools will you use to help ensure my success?

Q7. Will you use your own network to help me arrange informational or job interviews? (Note: The answer should be a definite Yes!)

Q8. Do you provide ALL of the following services?

- Comprehensive Background, Personality and Skills Review and Assessment
- Resume and Cover Letter Development
- LinkedIn Profile Development
- Value Statement (Elevator Pitch) Development
- Written Job Search Plan with Weekly Review (In-Person, Skype, or Phone)
- Informational and Job Interview Preparation
- Compensation Negotiation Consultation

Q9. Do you accept all job seekers who seek your services? (Note: the answer should be NO since a coach should not enter into a partnership with you if he perceives that you do not currently have the positive mental energy to put the necessary time and effort into your job search, or he feels you do not have the necessary chemistry to work together closely.)

Q10. Do you provide a FREE consultation, resume and LinkedIn profile review prior to entering into a coaching agreement? (Note: The answer should be Yes!)

A 30-minute job search strategy consultation with Steinfeld Coaching is FREE to readers of this book. To schedule, please use one of the following links:

Schedule Phone Call https://www.timetrade.com/book/WK11Q

Schedule Skype Call https://www.timetrade.com/book/BWDYM

Author Profiles

Steven Steinfeld

Steven Steinfeld is an acclaimed professional job search coach, speaker, and author. His job search seminars and workshops have been sponsored by many U.S. colleges and universities; and he has personally coached hundreds of international students in his one-to-one job search practice (www.steinfeldcoaching.com) and at the Business Schools of Northern Illinois University and the Illinois Institute of Technology (IIT). Steven is on multiple career related Advisory Boards and has consulted with Associated Colleges of Illinois. His innovative approaches have resulted in TV, newspaper and radio interviews on hiring trends and job search strategies.

Prior to becoming a career, job search and executive coach, Steven had a distinguished career in management and business consulting at U.S., India and China based companies, and led multi-cultural teams in more than 20 countries on six continents for gobal companies such as IBM. He brings much of his expertise in marketing and strategic planning, as well as the experience gained in hundreds of hiring decisions, to the simple and proven 3-step job search approach outlined in this books and workshops. Steven holds a BS in Psychology and a Certificate in Marketing Management from The Wharton School at the University of Pennsylvania.

Steven's profile, with well over 2000 unsolicited Endorsements, is among the top 1% viewed on LinkedIn. He invites you to get connected with him and email him your career and job search coaching question. You can learn more about him and his company by using the following links:

Website: http://steinfeldcoaching.com

LinkedIn: www.linkedin.com/in/stevensteinfeld

Email: steven@steinfeldcoaching.com

Media Profile: http://bit.ly/2dnIzrK

Author Profile: http://amzn.to/2kt6j0T

Sage Knowledge Video "Career Coaching" for Students - http://bit.ly/2fJDhYl

Yinping (Ping) Huang

Yinping (Ping) Huang **has been** an international student consultant to both International Student USA and InternshipDesk.

Ping graduated with a Master's degree in Public Administration (4.0 GPA) from Illinois Institute of Technology, (IIT) and was the Student Speaker at the 2013 IIT Stuart School of Business Commencement Ceremony. He earned his Bachelor of Management and Bachelor of Law degrees from the Beijing Institute of Technology with high honors in 2010. As an active student leader in college, he received the Beijing Youth Leader Award from the City of Beijing, China.

Ping has experience in program management and development, administration, operations, marketing and outreach, research, data analysis, and relationship management by virtue of his diverse work experiences at Google, the Mayor's Office of the City of Chicago, The U.S.-China Chamber of Commerce, The U.S.-China Exchange and Education Association, Illinois Institute of Technology, and China Merchants Bank.

Ron Cushing

Ron Cushing is the Director of International Services at the University of Cincinnatti and the Owner and Lead Trainer at Immigration Concepts. He is an International Education professional with over 20 years of experience that includes expertise in all aspects of international student and scholar services and recruitment. This includes serving as the Principle Designated School and Responsible Officer for SEVIS programs, submitting employment petitions and permanent resident petitions and verifying the employment eligibility of international workers.

Made in the USA
Middletown, DE
15 July 2019